Nevada

Yesterdays

Book Sponsors:

LAS VEGAS
REVIEW-JOURNAL

Nevada Yesterdays

Frank Wright

SHORT LOOKS AT LAS VEGAS HISTORY

Stephens Press ✦ Las Vegas, Nevada

Editor: A. D. Hopkins, Designer: Sue Campbell

ISBN 1-932173-27-7

CIP Data Available

A Stephens Media Group Company
Post Office Box 1600
Las Vegas, NV 89125-1600

www.stephenspress.com

Printed in Hong Kong

CONTENTS

Chapter ONE

Exploring Las Vegas Street Names ✦ The Gamble of
Dominguez and Escalante ✦ Mexican Traders Miss the Springs
✦ Jedediah Smith ✦ John C. Fremont ✦ A Valley Called Death
✦ The Killing of Archibald Stewart

Chapter TWO

The Clark-Harriman War ✦ The Golden Thumbtack ✦ Birth of a
Railroad Town ✦ The Race to Bullfrog ✦ Marooned! The Flood
of 1910 ✦ The Two Depots ✦ The Arrowhead Trail ✦ Railroad
Underpasses ✦ Highway 95 ✦ Las Vegas Streets ✦ Monorail,
Dream of the Future ✦ Las Vegas' First Airport ✦ Western Air
Express ✦ McCarran Airports ✦ Bonanza Airlines

Chapter THREE

The Bar of Justice ✦ Six Companies Versus Ed Krause ✦ The
Blue Room ✦ Sam Gay ✦ The Dugan Trial ✦ Bridget Waters
✦ Gun Law

Chapter FOUR

Prohibition ✦ Liberty's Last Stand ✦ End of Prohibition ✦ Divorce
Las Vegas Style ✦ Mr. Gormley's Divorce Problems ✦ "Ma" and
"Whataman": A Case Study ✦ Dude Ranches ✦ Marriage ✦
Keno Battles of the '30s ✦ Tony Cornero and the Meadows ✦
Guy McAfee and the Californians ✦ Senator Kefauver Looks
Down his Nose ✦ Vegas' Most Notorious Block

Chapter FIVE

Chapter SIX

Chapter SEVEN

Chapter EIGHT

Chapter NINE

Chapter TEN

Chapter ELEVEN

Chapter TWELVE

Chapter THIRTEEN

WHEN HISTORY HIT THE AIRWAVES

It's all about relationships. Personal friendships. Professional associations. Institutional partnerships. Connections between people. Connections between the past and the present. Links between the written word and the spoken word, and to the magical transformation into radio waves.

This book is the end product of all those points of contact, brought together by the singular vision of one extraordinary man — historian, teacher, writer, preservationist and friend Frank Wright.

Frank was without a doubt the go-to guy for local history. He was the quiet zealot whose accessibility and knowledge and enthusiasm enlightened generations of Las Vegans that local history did not begin with Bugsy Siegel.

With so many people moving into Southern Nevada, Frank and I believed that a local history series on public radio was a great way of educating all those new residents about the rich history of Nevada, beyond the rise of the modern casino era in the late 1940s. We began *Nevada Yesterdays* in 1987 as a joint project with the Nevada State Museum, researched and written by Frank Wright and voiced by Romulo Soldevilla.

It was a hit from the beginning. It won grant support from the Nevada Humanities Committee and garnered numerous local and national awards. Frank persistently kept churning out weekly episodes year after year in his popular style, often seasoned with vignettes of the colorful characters that pepper our desert west landscape.

Frank was our consultant on a 1991 two-part documentary KNPR produced on race relations in Las Vegas, called *Mississippi of the West or Promised Land?* That program aired on NPR's *All Things Considered* and won a Scripps Howard Award of Excellence. He was also our lead researcher on another award-winning history series we produced, called *The Las Vegas I Remember.* It featured first-person accounts by pioneer Las Vegans.

All of us at Nevada Public Radio are proud of our long association with Frank Wright. We are very pleased that Frank's widow, Dorothy, was able to finish what he began and that we had the pleasure to first broadcast. The program continues to this day with Michael Green writing and Senator Richard Bryan voicing.

Nevada Public Radio's mission is to enhance the quality of life and build a better community. Frank lived that mission. He made our community a richer and better place to live. His book continues his legacy, conveying to future generations his deep belief in the value of the past.

Lamar Marchese

KNPR President/General Manager

THREE DECADES SEEKING THE FACTS

Frank Wright has been physically gone from us for over a year and it's an understatement to say that both his memory and his work live on. As those of us from the Nevada State Museum & Historical Society perform our jobs within the greater Southern Nevada community, we are constantly reminded of the connections Frank made, the number of people he reached, and the history he exposed. With every contact, no matter if you are talking about the disposition of a building, the pedigree of a property, or some obscure facet of Nevada history, one expects the inevitable, "It's too bad Frank isn't here, he'd know about this."

Frank began work in 1970 as the Curator of Education at the Nevada State Museum & Historical Society. In this capacity, he was charged with producing educational units for schoolchildren in fourth and seventh grades. While developing these materials, he developed a strong interest in local history. This interest turned into consummate passion and Frank became increasingly visible in just about every historic preservation and community history project. He gave guided tours of historic Las Vegas and spoke about local history to hundreds of community groups. His passion, for liberally spreading the truth about local history, helped the Museum advance our educational mission. Frank was a touchstone for those just seeking simple facts as well as those trying to understand the complex, sometimes convoluted human connections, which comprise our local history.

The Nevada State Museum & Historical Society is grateful that Frank's passion will be produced in this tangible form, the compendium of *Nevada Yesterdays*, so that still more people in our community may better understand and embrace our rich, wonderful history.

Greta Brunschwyler

Director, Nevada State Museum
and Historical Society

FOREWORD

Remembering Frank Wright

I had a Las Vegas history question recently and out of reflex picked up the phone, then paused before punching the numbers.

For a moment I'd forgotten: No Frank Wright on the other end of the line to provide an encouraging word and a sparkling nugget of factual information about the real Las Vegas.

What will we do without this understated, excellent man?

You may be excused for being so caught up in the present that you don't have time to think about the past. But no society prospers long without learning from its history, and Wright played an integral role in the preservation and presentation of the incredible true Las Vegas story.

Las Vegas history, the real Las Vegas history, makes fops and fools of even the most sincere explorers. The city's story is riddled with blind alleys, dead ends, crazy twists, and outright fabrication.

More sweat has been spent in almost getting the Las Vegas story right than was generated in building Hoover Dam. For the most part, you can't fault the effort of the academic historian or journalistic scribbler. But with a few exceptions, the game efforts of the big-picture guys and the slice-of-life guys fall short of capturing the quicksilver truth of the incredible living mirage on the Mojave.

For the truth, the unvarnished stuff that is the fruit of a love's labor with a place and its people, Las Vegas needed Wright. He died April 25, 2003 just weeks before his sixty-fifth birthday.

His departure leaves Southern Nevada without its most devoted chronicler and collector of historical material. His departure begs a question best posed by State Assistant Administrator of Archives and Records Guy Rocha, Wright's colleague and counterpart in Northern Nevada: "How does institutional memory survive?"

In stable, established communities, there are multigenerational families and structured historical and genealogical societies to preserve the past, Rocha observes. Without vigilance, the history of a place is lost.

In booming areas full of transient folks and hyperbolic promoters, those stories tend to get lost entirely or twisted dramatically. With its endless mythmaking, Las Vegas is one such place. Wright's friend, KNPR Station Manager Lamar Marchese observed, "His most defining characteristic was his deep felt belief in the value of the past in a town that regularly celebrates destroying what little of it we have left."

That dedication is the only way a boomtown can avoid what Rocha calls a "bad case of community Alzheimer's."

"You have to have gatekeepers, people who somehow rise to the occasion to sustain the institutional memory," Rocha says. "For the most part, Frank was the go-to guy every day. Probably no one person did more to not only sustain the memory, but to try to ensure it's as accurate as possible."

Wright's love of the Las Vegas story shined through. His friend, Community College of Southern Nevada history professor Michael Green, wrote recently, "Frank could walk around downtown and tell you the architecture of each building, who lived in what building for how long, and probably the shoe size of each resident. He understood that knowing an area's history fosters a sense of community, that becoming mired in the past is bad but an understanding of that past is the only road to a worthwhile future. That's why he insisted upon the need to preserve the downtown railroad cottages and businesses, and the classic houses."

Even the most well-meaning citizens are revisionist historians. It's part of human nature to embellish, fuzz up the facts and recall events and people in larger-than-life terms. In that way, we're all natural-born newspaper columnists. "People get confused about the past," Rocha says. "People are either intentionally or unintentionally misled about the past. Some people have their own agendas and want to make heroes."

But with Frank Wright around as a history cop, there was no getting away with, for example, calling Bugsy Siegel the father of Las Vegas or even the originator of the Flamingo.

And people came and called from around the world to tap into the resource between Wright's ears. For scores of authors, journalists, screenwriters and academics, Wright made might. He was hired as curator of education by the Nevada State Museum and for years produced those wonderful "Nevada Yesterdays" programs on public radio station KNPR. At the time of his death from cancer he was still editing this collection of those broadcasts. They are sure to be essential reading for anyone who cherishes the truth behind the myth of this amazing place.

"When it comes to a knowledge of early Las Vegas history, Frank was Mr. Las Vegas," Rocha says.

Without Frank Wright or someone as devoted, how will we remember the real Las Vegas?

John L. Smith

John L. Smith, a lifelong resident of Southern Nevada, is a columnist for the *Las Vegas Review-Journal*, where a shorter version of this article appeared shortly after Wright's death. This version later appeared in *Touchstone*, the newsletter of the Nevada Humanities Committee.

PROLOGUE

Presumably, "Whiskey Pete" McIntyre still reclines in his slightly tilted desert grave out near Stateline, an empty bottle of whiskey tucked into his belt. The first *Nevada Yesterdays* episode, written in 1987, recalled Whiskey Pete's career as a bootlegger in the Prohibition era.

Since then many historical characters have paraded through this series, ranging from the Spanish padres of 1776 to Bugsy Siegel and friends in 1946. What was to have been a three-year radio series is still on the air.

The enterprise resists summing up. We have tried to look at ordinary people as well as those who made history on a grander scale — people such as "River Joe" Whitney, the most arrested man in Las Vegas, as well as his frequent jailer, Sheriff Sam Gay; labor union members as well as industrial giants like Six Companies and Basic Magnesium against which they struggled.

Our heroes have been a motley assortment of politicians, lawyers, prizefighters, thespians, architects, baseball players, musicians, rodeo riders, evangelists, and suffragettes. We have sought to make our pursuit of history more than trivial, to find in Nevada's yesterdays the germ of who we are and what we are today.

Frank Wright

Pioneering

Exploring Las Vegas Street Names

The railroad officials who founded Las Vegas had a somewhat sketchy understanding of Western history. In 1905, they named all but one of the original nine east-west streets for famous explorers. However, the connection of some of them to Southern Nevada was remote at best. Two downtown streets derive their names from the early 19th century explorations of the American Northwest by Meriwether Lewis and William Clark. Their expedition was of great importance in the opening of the West, but their route was far to the north of Nevada. Benjamin Bonneville and Jim Bridger didn't get much closer. Captain Bonneville, though immortalized in the writings of Washington Irving, was but a marginal figure in the Western fur trade. His trading post on Wyoming's Green River was so little used that it was nicknamed "Fort Nonsense."

Bridger, a famous mountain man and fur trader, is credited with many accomplishments, including the first explorations of the Great Salt Lake. His closest approach to Southern Nevada might have been a brief trapping foray along the Humboldt River in Northern Nevada. Two of Bridger's associates, more worthy of recognition in Southern Nevada, have yet to be memorialized in street names. Fur trapper Jedediah Smith made path-breaking explorations in Southern Nevada in the 1820s, and famed black mountain man Jim Beckwourth crossed through Las Vegas Valley a time or two in the 1840s.

Kit Carson and John C. Fremont. Kit Carson was Fremont's guide on the expedition that literally put Las Vegas on American maps.

Four of the downtown streets are named for explorers of genuine significance to Nevada. Hudson's Bay Company fur trapper Peter Skene Ogden was the first outsider to explore the length of the Humboldt River, and he traversed that region extensively. One epic trek in 1829, from Oregon to the Colorado River, likely brought him through or very close to Las Vegas Valley. Spaniard Francisco Garces blazed the western leg of the Old Spanish Trail to California, near the southern tip of the state, in 1776. Las Vegas' main thoroughfare is aptly named for John C. Fremont, who camped here in 1844 and mapped a later version of that trail through Las Vegas. The much-celebrated Kit Carson was Fremont's guide on the expedition that literally put Las Vegas on American maps. The ninth original street was named for Helen J. Stewart, who owned and managed the Las Vegas Ranch from 1884 until 1901.

The Gamble of Domínguez and Escalante

July 4, 1776. The Liberty Bell pealed in Philadelphia while half a continent away, in the Spanish province of New Mexico, Franciscan priests Francisco Dominguez and Silvestre Velez de Escalante lamented a delay in the commencement of their grand project. It was the day set for their departure on a trailblazing expedition that they hoped would lead to a suitable overland route from New Mexico to the new presidio at Monterey in Alta California.

Father Escalante's illness delayed them until July 29.

Then, Ute Indian guides helped the padres and their eight companions forge a sweeping route northwest from Santa Fe into the valley of Utah Lake in present day Utah. The expedition's cartographer, Don Bernardo Miera, drew remarkably accurate maps of this previously unexplored region. He did make errors that bedeviled posterity; his map showed two large rivers flowing westward toward San Francisco Bay. Fur trappers and explorers who came later searched long and fruitlessly for these great potential avenues of commerce.

Fremont Street in 1949. The street bears the name of the intrepid explorer.

By early October, Dominguez, Escalante, and the eight others were in dire trouble in their southwesterly course along the present route of Interstate 15 in what is now southwestern Utah. One day's journey of some 50 miles had been without water. The crisis eased the next day, as they found salty but potable water. On October 5, a cold wind sprang up, a foreboding of the snow that began on the sixth. As it became apparent that winter had set in, Domínguez and Escalante wisely thought better of attempting to complete the crossing to Monterey, still some 520 air miles distant. Don Bernardo, seeing glory and honor slipping from his grasp, grumbled openly, converting others to his view that they were but a week out from their destination.

The padres proposed a solution: they would solicit God's will by prayer, and by the casting of lots. On October 11, Divine Will confirmed the decision to return to Santa Fe. Once again in harmony, the party turned toward the Colorado River and home. What historians came to call the "Old Spanish Trail" was still more idea than reality. Had they continued on their original course, history might have credited them with the discovery of Las Vegas Valley. It is one of the gentler ironies of history that Las Vegas failed of discovery by a gamble.

Mexican Traders Miss the Springs

One of the chief delights of the study of history is that there are few immutable truths. Many historical "facts" turn out on closer examination to be misunderstandings. For example, it's more or less common "knowledge" that Las Vegas sat astride the Old Spanish Trail, which, in the nineteenth century, carried commerce between New Mexico and Southern California. Most historical maps attest to this. It *is* clear that Las Vegas was a watering stop on a trail, portions of which can still be discerned. But was it the Old Spanish Trail?

The first commercial caravan known to have passed through Las Vegas Valley was led by New Mexican merchant Antonio Armijo in early 1830. Armijo carried woven goods to exchange for California livestock. Careful research by Elizabeth Warren[1] demonstrates that Armijo's route barely skirted the southern edge of the valley. While trading caravans moved more or less regularly across the Mojave Desert for the next eighteen years, no other party is known to have used Armijo's route. Most bypassed Las Vegas altogether and instead traveled south, following the Colorado River to Needles, in present day California. From that point they followed a trail west, first marked by Spanish explorer Francisco Garces in 1776. That, properly speaking, should be called the Old Spanish Trail.

How then did it come to be understood that the Old Spanish Trail came through Las Vegas? American explorer John C. Fremont confidently but mistakenly assumed he was on the Old Spanish Trail in 1844 when he followed a rugged trail eastward over Mountain Springs Pass between Pahrump and Las Vegas Valley. He so recorded it in his report, which received wide distribution. When Americans carried Fremont's report and maps through the area in greater numbers over the next few years, they followed his route and his nomenclature. However, Fremont's trail through Las Vegas was neither old nor Spanish.

In many accounts of the first people of European heritage to pass through Las Vegas Valley, the name Rafael Rivera looms very large — maybe too large. According to legend, Rivera was the first non-native to view the valley. In truth, very little is actually known about him. In late 1829 and early 1830, Rivera served as a scout for the Armijo pack train. On Christmas Day 1829, according to Armijo's journal, the party camped on the Virgin River about a hundred miles northeast of Las Vegas. Rivera and several others departed on a reconnaissance mission. The scouting party returned a week later without Rivera. During that time, the main group had reached the Colorado River and was following it southward. On January 7, thirteen days after his departure, Rivera rejoined the others at the mouth of Las Vegas Wash. Where had Rivera been? He reported that he had recognized Mohave Indian villages and a crossing of the Colorado he had seen the year before. The villages and crossing were about ninety miles downriver from Las Vegas.

Armijo chose not to follow Rivera's path. Instead, he led the party westward, passing through what is now Green Valley. Their only two overnight stops in or near Las Vegas Valley were dry camps. The record clearly indicates that Rivera had not seen, let alone named, Las Vegas Springs, as many history books incorrectly claim. It was some later and as yet unidentified party that would happen upon the springs and record the place as The Meadows on Mexican maps.

Why go to into such detail to revise a historical interpretation? Because without constant rethinking, bad information can become the basis of popular belief.

Jedediah Smith

Only twenty-seven years old, Jedediah Smith was, by 1826, already a legend in the fledgling American fur trade in the Rocky Mountains. Two years earlier, the Bible-toting mountain man had earned his place in American history as the discoverer of South Pass, that broad highway through the Rockies for later thousands of Oregon- and California-bound

Jedediah Smith

emigrants. In the late summer of 1826, he was about to add to his list of achievements. Searching for new fur trapping areas, he had arrived at the Virgin River of what is now southwestern Utah. For part of his route, he had followed in the footsteps of the Domínguez-Escalante expedition of almost exactly fifty years earlier.

Unlike his Franciscan predecessors who veered off toward Santa Fe, Smith continued down the Virgin to its juncture with the Colorado. He thereby became the first American to enter the territory of the present state of Nevada. By October, Smith and a handful of companions were in a race with starvation as they struggled through rugged terrain along the east bank of the Colorado. Having lost half of their horses and fearing for their lives, they finally reached help at the Mojave

Indian villages near the present site of Needles, California.

After fifteen days of recuperation, Smith traded with the Mojaves for supplies and fresh horses and then struck westward over an ages-old Indian trade route to the southern coast of California. Again he trod where a Spanish padre had earlier passed. In 1776, Francisco Garces had been guided over the same route from the Colorado to San Gabriel Mission. Smith's trek forged the key central link in what became known as the Old Spanish Trail, fulfilling the dream of the Spanish explorers of 1776.

John C. Fremont

In the 1840s and 1850s, John C. Fremont explored much of Nevada and named many of the state's most prominent geographical features. His name and that of his famous guide, Kit Carson, are memorialized by street names in downtown Las Vegas.

In 1844, Fremont led a large exploring party on the last leg of a thirty-five-hundred-mile trek around that vast western region he

---

[**1840**]　　　　[**1860**]　　　　[**1880**]

1848 GOLD DISCOVERED IN CALIFORNIA

HOMESTEAD ACT OF 1862 (REPEALED IN 1976)
CIVIL WAR 1861—1865
1873 FINANCIAL PANIC

1826
Jedediah Smith enters Nevada region.

1830
Armijo caravan travels through Las Vegas Valley.

1844
John C. Fremont camps in Las Vegas.

1846
Donner party tragedy, Sierra Nevada Mountains.

1849
California gold rush begins.

1860–80s
Silver and gold draw miners to Nevada.

1860
The first bank opens in Nevada.

The first mill built in Galena, Nevada for processing ore from the Comstock Lode.

1864
Nevada becomes a state.

1869
John Wesley Powell expedition runs the length of the Grand Canyon in boats.

1867
U.S. purchases Alaska terrritory from Russia.

1884
Archibald Stewart is killed.

1889
50,000 Oklahoma settlers rush to claim former Indian lands given away by Federal Government.

1890
U.S. Census Bureau deems the Western frontier closed and settled.

1900
Alaskan Klondike, Canandian Yukon draw 60,000 gold miners.

President McKinley signs bill adopting the gold standard to measure the value of the dollar.

Many miners died on the dangerous trail to Dawson, Alaska.

John C. Fremont

called the Great Basin. His journal entry for May 3 gives us one of our earliest glimpses of Las Vegas. "We camped," he said, "at a camping ground called Las Vegas — a term which the Spanish use to signify fertile or marshy plains. Two narrow streams of clear water, four or five feet deep, gush suddenly with a quick current, from two singularly large springs. They afforded a delightful bathing place."

Fremont and his party camped but one night at Las Vegas. On May 4, they resumed their journey toward the region that is now northern Utah. Fremont kept meticulous records of the route they followed. Their path after leaving the area of Nevada was, in fact, a variant of the Old Spanish Trail begun by the Spanish Fathers, Domínguez and Escalante, in 1776. The widely circulated report of the expedition was of major importance to the future development of Southern Nevada. Three years later, Fremont's trail became an important route between southern California and the new Mormon community of Salt Lake City. In 1855, a small party of men from Salt Lake made the first attempt to create a permanent settlement at Las Vegas, Fremont's camping spot of eleven years earlier.

A Valley Called Death

"Never take no cut offs and hurry along as fast as you can." This was advice to future overland emigrants given by a thirteen-year-old survivor of the tragic Donner-Reed Party of 1846. If the large party of forty-niners camped along the Old Spanish Trail in early November 1849 had heard the advice, they chose to ignore it.

One of them produced a map showing a shortcut to California across the desert north of Las Vegas. Their Mormon guide, Jefferson Hunt, a hardened veteran of the customary trail, advised them against the untried route. "I believe you will get into the jaws of hell," he warned. Only twenty-seven wagons followed Hunt south along the known route. The majority, with a hundred wagons and many pack animals, turned westward into the unknown.

Among this group was a young trapper named William Manly, who was headed for the California gold fields with his friends, the Bennett family.

The sheer walls of Beaver Dam Wash soon blocked their advance. After three days of futile exploration, most of the emigrants left the spot they called Mount Misery and retraced their steps to follow Hunt toward Las Vegas. A few abandoned their wagons and trekked down the wash and linked up later with Hunt at the Muddy River. The others,

---

[1900]   [1920]   [1940]

WORLD WAR I 1914—1919   THE GREAT DEPRESSION   US IN WORLD WAR II 1941—1945

1902
Helen Stewart sells Las Vegas Ranch.

1905
Auction of the Las Vegas town site.

1910
Nevada population fewer than two people per square mile.

U.S. population hits 91.6 million. Urban pop. exceeds rural for first time.

1928
President Hoover signs the Boulder Canyon Act, by 1931 thousands of unemployed people come looking for work on the dam construction project.

1935
FDR dedicates Hoover Dam. (Then called Boulder Dam.)**1941**

Army Air Force gunnery school opens in Las Vegas.

1946
Baby boom begins as war veterans return, marry and start families.

U.S. housing-starts up from 144,000 to 1.7 million.

1947
Nevada Legislature creates the Las Vegas Valley Water District.

1948
Second McCarran Airport on the south Strip opens.

1949
The gunnery school is re-activated as Nellis AFB.

1950
Population of Southern Nevada grows to 6-18 people per square mile. (entire state: 160,083 persons)

U.S. population 151 million.

1959
Las Vegas Convention Center opens.

1963
Voters approve bonds for current McCarran Airport.

1969
Corporate Gaming OK'd by state legistlature.

1980
Las Vegas area population is 45-90 per square mile. (Nevada's population: 798,523)

2004
Las Vegas is 2.3 million, people; is the fastest growing city in U.S. for the eighteenth year.

USA population reaches 295 million.

with twenty-seven wagons, struck out over a forbidding route to the north and west.

On November 21, Jefferson Hunt and his charges reached safety at the oasis of Las Vegas. About the same time, and nearly dead from thirst, those who had continued on the cutoff approached Papoose Dry Lake on the edge of what became the Nevada Test Site. They called it Misery Lake. Disheartened and demoralized, they splintered into several smaller groups. These pioneers were to face many more trials before stumbling by diverse routes into a valley that takes its name from their suffering — Death Valley.

The Reverend John Brier, with his wife and three young sons, trailed behind a group of men calling themselves the Jayhawkers. Manly, the Bennetts, and other families struck off in another direction.

In late December, the Jayhawkers, followed by the Briers, crossed the Funeral Mountains into Death Valley. Mrs. Brier later described that Christmas Eve: "Night came on," she said, "and we lost all track of those ahead. I would get down and look in the starlight for the ox tracks and we would stumble on." Christmas dinner the next evening was ox meat, black coffee and a little bread.

Meanwhile, Manly's group came upon the Brier trail and the young man faced a powerful temptation. Scouting ahead, Manly knew he could push on alone and save himself. Instead, he led his charges to the Briers' recently vacated Christmas camp. Enduring almost incredible hardship, the Briers finally reached help at a California rancho on February 4. Manly and another man had already been there and heroically returned to Death Valley with supplies for the Bennetts and others still stranded. Barely alive, that part of the original party emerged from the desert in early March. Without William Manly's Christmas Eve resolve, they would surely have perished.

Archibald and Helen Stewart

The Killing of Archibald Stewart

On July 13, 1884, Archibald Stewart returned to his Las Vegas Ranch from a business trip to the mining camps at Eldorado Canyon. In his absence, his wife, Helen, had words with one Schyler Henry, a disgruntled hired hand. Demanding, but not receiving his pay, Henry announced that he was quitting and set out for Conrad Kiel's ranch a couple of miles north.

Mrs. Stewart told her husband of the quarrel upon his return. After eating and resting, Archibald threw his rifle on his shoulder and rode away, but Mrs. Stewart saw no reason for alarm, because he did not appear to be heading in the direction of the Kiel Ranch and potential trouble.

A short time later, a scrawled note arrived. "Mrs. Sturd. Send a team and take Mr. Sturd away. He is dead." The note was signed "C. Kiel."

Archibald Stewart

Sadly, Mrs. Stewart buried her husband the next day in a casket made of the wooden doors of the ranch house. Apart from old Conrad Kiel and Schyler Henry, there were apparently no other witnesses to the shooting. Outlaw Hank Parrish, who would be hanged for a later murder, was known to have been in the area but could not be found. At the inquest, Henry claimed self-defense. Stewart had run toward him, he said, and had shot first. An exchange of gunfire left Henry wounded and Stewart dead.

What really happened that July 13? Did Stewart intend to confront Henry about the quarrel and be-come instead a victim himself? Or was he, as Mrs. Stewart believed, lured to his death? Whatever really happened, Helen Stewart was left to raise a family and operate the ranch herself until its sale in 1902 led to the founding of Las Vegas.

Chapter Notes

[1] Elizabeth von Till Warren, *Armijo's trace revisited: A new interpretation of the impact of the Antonio Armijo Route of 1829-1830 on the development of the Old Spanish Trail*

Helen Stewart in later years.

Chapter TWO

Trains, Planes and Automobiles

The Clark-Harriman War

Not long after the completion of the transcontinental railroad in 1869, the Union Pacific Railroad thought to build through Nevada into Southern California. Work actually started in 1890, but it just wasn't to be. The Union Pacific went into bankruptcy in the Panic of 1893.

Two events in August 1900 led to the revival of the idea. Collis P. Huntington of the Southern Pacific Railroad died, and E.H. Harriman of the Union Pacific seized the opportunity to rejuvenate his own company with a large purchase of Southern Pacific stock. Also that month, Senator William Andrews Clark of Montana purchased a small railroad at the Port of Los Angeles and a "paper" railroad in Utah. His intention to challenge Harriman's new monopoly was clear. The two-year Clark-Harriman War was about to begin.

Both companies began grading. With a right-of-way granted by the Nevada Legislature, Senator Clark had the law on his side. But by paying extravagant wages of twenty dollars a day, the Union Pacific had more men in the field. The first battles were fought with shovels at the Utah-Nevada line in April 1901. Even Clark's lawyer, C.O. Whittemore, wielded a shovel, but it was not enough. Despite heroic resistance, the Clark men were driven from the field by thirty-two charging wagons and a mule team.

The Lincoln County Sheriff enforced a truce that held until November 1901 when all work mysteriously ceased for two years. Just as mysteriously, grading work resumed in 1903. Not until much later was it revealed that Clark and

Harriman had swung a joint ownership deal. The way was finally cleared for the completion of the railroad and the founding of Las Vegas two years later.

Above: William A. Clark
Below: E.H. Harriman

The Golden Thumbtack

On January 30, 1905, a small freighting-and-construction camp called Las Vegas celebrated Railroad Day. Ordinarily, the completion of a railroad and the symbolic driving of a golden spike was an occasion for jubilation in an isolated Western community. Townsfolk usually gave over an entire day to parades, sporting events, banquets, and much wining and dining.

On that wintry afternoon thirty miles south of Las Vegas, by contrast, the ceremony was brief and perfunctory. But then the golden spike wasn't much either. In the rush to complete the San Pedro, Los Angeles and Salt Lake Railroad, only the wife of the road's general manager gave much thought to the ceremonial niceties. She had arranged to have a miniature gold spike made.

After a Greek laborer drove the last real spike, the chief engineer fished this tiny ornament out of his vest pocket and drove it into a railroad tie with a tack hammer. The Mexican, Greek, Italian, and Austrian immigrants who largely made up the work crews cheered briefly as the first locomotive rolled over the completed track. The ceremony was over. Four months later and thirty miles to the north, an auction officially inaugurated Las Vegas as a service center for the railroad.

Today, a historical marker labeled "The Last Spike," stands in the desert off Interstate 15, 4.6 miles northeast of Jean, commemorating the significant event more memorably than the brief ceremony of a century ago.

Birth of a Railroad Town

There is a long tradition of Las Vegas-bashing by the national media. In the 1930s and '40s, magazines and press services averred that Las Vegas was a place where sin was a civic virtue, a place whose gambling dens and liquor joints seduced young couples into marriage while intoxicated. Las Vegas was, according to one story, "the cesspool of the West." In 1906, even the editor of the little *Rhyolite Herald* sneered that few people would hesitate to take the first train out of town.

The first press smearing of Las Vegas, in fact, came on Day One of the city's existence in May 1905. A *Los Angeles Examiner* reporter named Pierson attended the auction that launched Las Vegas. Drinking beer he said had been boiled in the sun for a week, Pierson strolled the new town site. He described for his readers the freighters, prospectors, miners and tinhorns elbowing their way through the hot streets, listening to the tuneless banging of the town's one piano. In Pierson's view, it was these desert dwellers, willing to gamble on anything, who bid up the prices on lots, hoping to make a killing in thirty days. As for the future of Las Vegas, he opined that the lots could be repurchased within a year, with good buildings on them, for less than the price of the ground.

Then, as now, the local press response was vociferous. It was greedy Angelenos who bid up the prices, whereas local bidders were earnest businessmen and homebuilders. There were several excellent

Las Vegas townsite auction held May 15, 1905.

pianos in town and, for the record, the beer was ice cold.

Less widely known is the fact that a town named Las Vegas existed well before the auction was held. Already a sizeable railroad construction camp in late summer 1904, Las Vegas grew by year's end into a major freighting center for the newly discovered Rhyolite gold mines.

In January 1905, surveyor J.T. McWilliams filed the first plat map for the town and called it the "Original Las Vegas Town site." "McWilliams Town," as folks called it, was west of the railroad tracks, the area long afterward called West Las Vegas. McWilliams advertised his town extensively in California newspapers, "Do not be misled," he warned, "by false report as to the location of the real town site," Some, undoubtedly, were misled by the ad itself, and purchased lots they assumed were in the railroad town site, which was not yet platted.

McWilliams's gamble to make his town site the business center of Las Vegas was doomed to failure. When the railroad finally held its auction in May, the Original Las Vegas Town Site was rapidly depopulated in favor of the new town east of the tracks. A fire that destroyed the area's business district in September only sealed the inevitable. Long neglected thereafter, West Las Vegas was to play a significant part in the growth of the Las Vegas community in the 1940s.

The Race to Bullfrog

In September 1905, Las Vegas became the focus of a clash between two industrial titans. One of the combatants was Francis M. Smith, a one-time drifter and prospector who parlayed an 1872 discovery of borax ores into the presidency of his own giant company, maker of "20-Mule Team

This passenger railcar served as the train station at the time of the townsite auction in 1905.

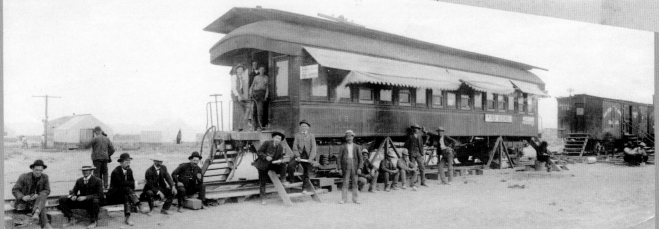

Borax." The other industrialist was William A. Clark, builder of the Los Angeles to Salt Lake railroad. Clark had started out as a prospector in Montana in 1863. By the turn of the century, he had amassed a huge fortune in mining, smelting, and banking. He served as the president, board of directors, and sole stockholder in fourteen immense corporations.

According to one account, the maneuvering began in April with a chance meeting between the two men in San Francisco. Over brandy and cigars they struck a deal — or so Smith thought. Clark persuaded Smith to alter his railroad plans; Smith had incorporated the To-nopah & Tidewater Railroad to connect the new Bullfrog Mining District and his own borax mine near Death Valley to the Santa Fe Railroad in Southern California. Instead, Clark offered a connection to his own line at Las Vegas. This would shorten the route for the borax magnate and gain for himself freight tonnage from the mines. The two shook hands on the arrangement.

By July, T&T crews were working near Las Vegas. In August, they were stopped short, halted by a court order banning trespass on Clark property. Clark had reneged, airily dismissing the San Francisco conversation as not a binding agreement. He was going to build his own railroad to Bullfrog. Smith was unfazed. In September, he proceeded with his original plan to build from California as Clark announced plans to build the Las Vegas & Tonopah Railroad. The race to Bullfrog was on.

Smith, building from Ludlow, California, got an early start but stalled hopelessly in rugged Amargosa Canyon. Clark's LV&T reached the Bullfrog Mining District at Beatty in December 1906, easily winning the race. The following April, yet another railroad, the little Bullfrog-Goldfield, arrived in Beatty from the north. Nevada

Wagons loaded with supplies line up for the trip to the Bullfrog Mining District.

Block 16 - Freight Loaded for Delivery to Rhyolite -1907- Las Vegas

[1860]   [1900]   [1920]

CIVIL WAR 1861—1865   1873 FINANCIAL PANIC   WORLD WAR I 1914—1919   PROHIBITION 1920—1933

STOCK MARKET CRASH 1929

1869
Transcontinental Railroad completed with the Golden Spike at Promontory, Utah. It is lauded as the greatest accomplishement of the nineteenth century.

1870
The first train robbery in the Western United States

1903
Wright brothers first powered airplane flight at Kitty Hawk, N.C.

1905
Completion of The San Pedro, Los Angeles & Salt Lake RR is celebrated with the "Golden Thumbtack."

1905
Las Vegas Townsite Auction is held.

1906
Clark wins race to build railroad to Bullfrog– Goldfield Mine District.

1908
Ford Model T goes into wide production.

1910
New Year's flood. One hundred miles of track lost, suspending service for six months.

1912
The "unsinkable" Titanic luxury liner strikes iceberg; sinks in the North Atlantic.

1914
Panama Canal completed and opened.

1916
Travel writer C.H. Bigelow dubs the road from L.A. to Salt Lake, "Arrowhead Trail" and drives it in his Packard Twin Six "Cactus Kate."

1917
America enters WWI.

1925
Freemont Street is the first Las Vegas street paved.

1927
Charles Lindbergh completes first solo trans-Atlantic flight, New York to Paris.

now had a north-south rail connection, but a traveler from Reno to Las Vegas would have to ride over the tracks of five railroads to complete the trip.

The Senator's victory proved hollow. A national financial panic and depleted ore bodies caused the Bullfrog balloon to deflate after 1907. The LV& T lost money after its first year and hung on only until 1918. Borax Smith's Tonopah and Tidewater triumphed, surviving through World War II before finally folding in 1947.

Marooned!
The Flood of 1910

The auguries for the little town of Las Vegas were all positive on New Year's Eve 1909. The population stood at about fifteen hundred and was expected to double within a year. Workers of the San Pedro, Los Angeles, and Salt Lake Railroad were building sixty-four concrete-block cottages downtown. The comfortable modern homes were to house the families of the four hundred or so men who would come to town when the new railroad shops were completed. Exuberant reports of new artesian wells coming in almost weekly gave credence to claims that Las Vegas had unlimited agricultural potential.

On that rainy last day of 1909, the eastbound Los Angeles Limited pulled into the station on time. It was not to reach Salt Lake City for nearly six months. A downpour had set in motion a series of flash floods that wiped out a hundred miles of track in Meadow Valley Wash northeast of Las Vegas and also cut service to Los Angeles. The washout had come as a complete surprise: after a disastrous flood in 1907, the railroad had raised the roadbed through Meadow Valley Wash by four feet. It was a surprise, that is, to everyone except an old Paiute, who, three years earlier, had pointed far up on the canyon wall to show the high-water mark. The engineer in charge of construction had only laughed and pointed lower. The 1910 flood crest surpassed that of 1907 by a full eight feet.

Essentially marooned during the long reconstruction, Las Vegans began to realize their dependence on the railroad. Immediate layoffs created a severe slump in the local economy. The census taker reported that year that, far from growing as expected, the population had dwindled to under a thousand.

Clark County Review

VOLUME 2, NUMBER 2 · Las Vegas, Nevada, Saturday, January 8, 1910 · $2.00 PER YEAR, 5¢ PER COPY

Salt Lake Will Probably Abandon Rainbow Canyon Route

Meadow Valley Wash Again Exacts Tribute

Moapa Valley Ranches Completely Submerged

Million and a Half Dollars Spent on Last Washout Swept Away in a Twinkling and Devastation is Greater Than Ever

Meadow Valley Flood in Mad Rush for the Colorado Ruins Property and Endangers Lives. Virgin is also Raging

Las Vegas railyards with machine shops.

[1930] [1940] [1950]

GREAT DEPRESSION

JAPANESE ATTACK PEARL HARBOR, U.S. ENTERS WWII

POST-WAR ECONOMIC BOOM

1931
Las Vegas get its first traffic light on Fremont Street.

1935
One hundred cars a day drive the road that later becomes Highway 95.

1935
DC-3 Airliner revolutionizes air travel.

1937
Clark Avenue. (Bonanza Road) underpass opens.

1940
New Union Pacific Depot opens. First air-conditioned depot in U.S.

1941
Pearl Harbor attacked. U.S. enters WWII.

1956
Congress funds the Federal Highway Act. Construction begins on the U.S. Interstate Highway System. (Construction is expected to reach final completion in 2006.) Interstates cover 46,000 miles.

1961
Soviet Union puts first man in space.

1969
U.S. lands first men on the moon. Neil Armstrong is the first man to set foot there.

1997
The first supersonic land speed record (766 mph) set in Nevada's Black Rock Desert 125 miles north of Reno.

The slump ended abruptly in June 1910 when the entire town turned out to wave the Limited through on the rebuilt track. The railroad shops opened a few months later and the town experienced its first burst of growth as hundreds of new families arrived.

Unrealistic dreams of an agricultural paradise were forgotten in the Hoover Dam construction frenzy of the early 1930s. The railroad shops were torn down in the '20s and the remaining railroad buildings disappeared over the last few years. One of the original cottages for railroad workers can be visited at the Clark County Museum off Boulder Highway in Henderson.

Meadow Valley Wash was usually high and dry, but the flood of 1910 made this a raging torrent, ripping out tracks, stranding Las Vegas residents and cutting off supply lines to the north.

The Two Depots

In the spring of 1939, all of Las Vegas was excited about "Union Pacific — the movie, not the railroad. Cecil B. DeMille's extravaganza was set to premiere in Omaha, timed to coincide with the seventieth anniversary of the driving of the Golden Spike. Many of the cast — George Raft, Lloyd Nolan, Brian Donlevy, and even the great DeMille himself — boarded an unusual train at Los Angeles for the long haul to Nebraska. The train consisted of two of the newest steam-electric streamliners teamed up with an 1874 wood-burning locomotive, another star of the film. Four thousand Las Vegans, duded up in Helldorado costumes and accompa-

nied by bands and a motorcycle escort, greeted the Hollywood entourage at the Las Vegas depot.

That 1905 Mission-style structure at the head of Fremont Street had been at the center of community life for nearly forty years. An afternoon's diversion in the small railroad town might consist of a leisurely late lunch in the Union Pacific dining room — fondly called the "Beanery" — and a gander at

arriving passengers on the number 14 from Los Angeles. But by 1939, even the decorative lights strung out for the arrival of the celebrities couldn't hide the fact that the depot was a disgrace. The hullabaloo over the movie was its last hurrah. Railroad officials announced that it would be replaced. In June, the Beanery was closed to accommodate ticketing and baggage operations

The original mission style Union Pacific depot served passengers from 1905 to 1939.

The 1940 depot featured streamlined Moderne architecture. It boasted the distinction of being the first air-conditioned train terminal in the U.S. when it opened.

while the old station was being demolished.

The new terminal of 1940 was a far cry from the old. With its sweeping curves and soaring tower, the Art Moderne structure resembled nothing so much as one of the 90 mile-per-hour streamliner locomotives just then coming into service. The tower was more than a decorative element; it housed the refrigeration equipment for the first air-conditioned terminal in America. As forward-looking as the depot was, there wasn't much future to look forward to. Railroad passenger service declined precipitately in the 1960s. On May 1, 1971, the once-magnificent *City of Los Angeles*, the UP's sole surviving passenger train, made its last run. On its last car was the hand-lettered sign, "Adios." Eight years elapsed before Amtrak resumed passenger service over the line in 1979.

The Arrowhead Trail

At the dawn of the twentieth century, there were about 8,000 registered automobiles in the United States. A decade later, there were nearly half a million. Across the country, Main Street merchants combined with auto and tire manufacturers to lobby powerfully for better roads. The lobbies often took the form of highway associations. One of the earliest was the Lincoln Highway Association whose efforts, beginning in 1912, resulted in the first coast-to-coast highway.

Southern Nevada was not to be outdone in the scramble for a highway. In April 1913, Las Vegas dignitaries met with officials in Salt Lake City to drum up support for an "All-the-Year" road between Los

Angeles and the Utah capital. The Las Vegas Chamber of Commerce and the local newspaper took up the cause, as did the Automobile Club of Southern California. Newspaper articles touted the scenic beauties of the existing road northeast from Las Vegas. St. Thomas residents helped the cause by scratching away at a route through the Valley of Fire. By 1915, a group of Las Vegas excursionists could boast that they had traveled the fifty-seven miles to St. Thomas in just four hours without mishap.

A big boost for the road through Las Vegas came in 1916 from none other than "Cactus Kate." Cactus Kate[1] was actually a "Twin-Six" Packard automobile driven by noted travel writer C.H. Bigelow. With his widely read reports of his travels, Bigelow single-handedly popularized the route and gave it the name by which it was known for many years: the Arrowhead Trail. Unlike its modern descendant, Interstate 15, the Arrowhead Trail did not head directly for Barstow via Jean and State Line. Travelers who challenged the desert in those early years drove south to Searchlight and Needles where they picked up the route that became the legendary Route 66. Not many were up to the challenge. Fully a decade after Bigelow's trip, traffic on the Arrowhead Trail averaged only about 200 cars per day.

Railroad Underpasses

The opening of a railroad underpass is ordinarily not an occasion for great festivity. But the underpass on Clark Avenue in Las Vegas was opened in 1937 with one of the city's largest celebrations ever. Lieutenant Governor Fred Alward led a grand parade from Sixth Street to the west portal of the new structure. There, politicians, business and labor leaders, and railroad dignitaries orated at great length.

Why the hullabaloo? Clark Avenue, now renamed Bonanza, was part of the Tonopah-Reno highway and served as the major link between the business center of Las Vegas and "West Las Vegas." For thirty-two years, the railroad tracks had effectively separated West Las Vegas, the "Original Las Vegas Town Site," from the rest of the city. The $200,000 federally funded underpass now symbolically united the two parts of the community. Unfortunately, the wartime emergency of the early 1940s quickly demonstrated the inadequacy of the new route. Huge trucks carrying magnesium ore from west central Nevada to the huge defense plant at Henderson had great difficulty negotiating the low and narrow new underpass.

Because of low property values and a sparse population, civic amenities came very slowly to West Las Vegas. In the 1930s, Las Vegas used New Deal funds to upgrade the town's sewer system, pave its streets, and build parks, but West Las Vegas was largely passed over. With the new underpass linking them to the rest of Las Vegas, Westside residents hoped that these improvements would be forthcoming. They would be urgently needed.

Las Vegas Review-Journal

This underpass on Bonanza is still in use today. Built in 1937, it united the business district with West Las Vegas.

In the early 1940s, a severe wartime housing shortage hit Las Vegas. Hundreds of new families, many of them African-American, sought work in local defense industries. Not finding suitable housing except in West Las Vegas, they strained available services to the breaking point. Simultaneously, Las Vegas rapidly evolved into a strictly segregated society. The concrete underpass, celebrated so recently as a unifying element in the city, was now seen as a barrier, a "Concrete Curtain." The structure is still there, of course, just west of Main. When you drive under it, note the simple 1930s Art Deco touches.

In mid-1943, state highway officials made the decision to extend the Tonopah Highway south to Charleston Boulevard over what was to become Rancho Road. One thing they couldn't decide then was whether to create an underpass or an overpass on Charleston. In the end, they did neither; the seventy-foot behemoths, with their loads of magnesium ore, simply bumped over the rails.

It wasn't until well after the closing of the magnesium plant and the end of the war that highway officials finally decided upon the present underpass. And even then, Charleston was widened to four lanes only because indignant residents pointed out the inordinate number of accidents at the Bonanza crossing. Perhaps an underpass was the wrong way to go. The concrete was hardly dry on the structure when state highway engineers threw up their hands and declared the flooding problem practically unsolvable. But this will come as no surprise to generations of soggy commuters confronting Lake Charleston while trying to get home in a downpour.

Highway 95

Las Vegas was born in 1905 on the cusp of the golden age of railroads and the emerging era of the automobile. It was hard to get to the state capitol at Carson City by either mode of transportation. In 1907 a direct rail link was completed, but even then the trip wasn't recommended. An intrepid Reno-bound traveler would have to embark on the Las Vegas and Tonopah Railroad

U.S. 95 in Las Vegas at the "Spaghetti Bowl."

and make at least two transfers to other railroads.

A trip by car through the desert sand was even more frightful. As early as 1905, the Western Motor Car Company attempted to subdue the desert. They sent an automobile as far north as Beatty to test both car and road. The one-way trip took twenty hours and the car didn't survive. A fleet of rugged new White autos met similar defeat and the company declared the road a failure.

A great opportunity came in 1919 when the LV& T tore up its tracks and sent the rails to Shanghai. E.W. Griffith, a state senator from Las Vegas, introduced a bill that year providing that the state should acquire the railroad bed for a highway. The governor signed the bill in February, and by August, crews had graded about thirty miles of the new road. The state highway department promised one of the best roads in the state.

Nearly a year later, a disgusted Clark County Commission opined that the new road was worse than the old. A journal kept by a traveler that year tended to bear this out. The trip started on Main Street, then went west for three miles along the present route of Bonanza. From there, there were no road signs. A right turn at what is now Rancho Road put one on the old railroad right-of-way. One section of the road seemed typical: "turn to the left," the traveler said, "along the wire fence to corner; turn cross creek; keep to the left one mile to end of fence; sand. Subject to change as season advances."

The road improved only very gradually over the years, but by 1935 over a hundred cars traveled it every day. That primitive set of tire tracks evolved to become U.S. Highway 95.

Las Vegas Streets

The aggravation of long traffic delays occasioned by street construction is an unchangeable fact of modern city life. Not so in early Las Vegas. In the first place, there were not that many streets to keep up. In the second place, maintenance was taken care of by annually dousing the deeply rutted dirt thoroughfares with crankcase oil. That, and a futile sprinkling of water now and again to keep the dust down.

Las Vegas got its first paved street in 1925. Thirty horses provided the motive power for the heavy equipment that paved Fremont Street from Main to Fifth. Simultaneously, the nineteen-year-old redwood curbing was replaced with concrete, and North Main Street got a fresh coat of gravel. Fremont Street might have looked pretty spiffy, but the rest of the streets and alleys were a disgrace. Some were simply impassable by all but the sturdiest motorcars.

The *Review-Journal* editorialized in 1930 that the "main streets of the city are not half so presentable as

Fremont Street was first paved in 1925 from Main to Fifth. The welcome sign was hung to greet visiting dignitaries on their way to the Boulder Dam site in 1930.

the average well-kept garbage dump of the larger cities." By that first year of the Great Depression, the aesthetic problem was easily solvable. Local law enforcement officers simply rounded up a few vagrants, of whom there were plenty, and impressed them into a chain gang armed with brooms and shovels.

Early the next year, as construction on Boulder Dam got underway, the city experienced its first traffic jams. Tie-ups caused by double-parked cars were said to have created a "nightmare" on Fremont Street. Be that as it may, Las Vegas didn't get its first traffic signal until ten years later when the first light went up at Fremont and Las Vegas Boulevard. Lights at the other Fremont Street intersections came at regular intervals.

What about those double-parked cars? The city hoped to take care of that in 1942 by installing parking meters. That plan came to naught when the U.S. War Production Board wouldn't permit the use of critical metal. It wasn't until 1948, when the city put in over seven hundred meters, that Las Vegas motorists learned to live with that other constant of modern city life.

Monorail, Dream of the Future

In the year 2000, the state Board of Finance authorized the issuance of bonds that would lead to the expansion of the monorail system on the Las Vegas Strip. Peering into the dim future, planners suggested that the system would ultimately link McCarran Airport with the Strip and Fremont Street. The idea has been around for quite a while — remember the late, lamented People Mover of the 1980s? In fact, the dream is older than that.

In 1966, Lockheed Aircraft Corporation and Guerdon Industries, both well-endowed outfits, unveiled a visionary plan they dubbed "Magi-Cab." Renderings of the project showed a series of graceful arches suspending a monorail network above earthlings on the sidewalk below. Transportation stations, designed in a sort of post-Sputnik-Moderne style architecture, perched like eagles' aeries at intervals along the route.

Architecturally, the plan was the creation of influential Los Angeles architect Paul R. Williams. Williams, an African-American, had already left a mark on Las Vegas in the 1940s and 1950s. Among other projects, he had designed the Carver Park worker's housing tract near the Henderson magnesium plant, the short-lived Royal Nevada Hotel and Casino on the Las Vegas Strip, and the Las Vegas Downs racetrack behind the Thunderbird Hotel.

The system was to be an electronic marvel. Four-passenger cars would travel at twenty-five mph and depart from McCarran every thirteen seconds. With the push of a button, Magi-Cab passengers could be shunted off the main track automatically at any one of fifteen stations. Best of all, the seventeen-million-dollar project would be financed by private funds. If we had shelled out that seventeen million thirty-four years ago, would our Buck Rogers future have arrived already?

Las Vegas' First Airport

From 1920, when the first airplane touched down at Las Vegas, it took just twenty-nine years for the emerging resort to be just eleven and a half hours flying time from New York. The breathtaking growth of air travel goes far toward explaining Las Vegas' phenomenal development.

America emerged from World War I with thousands of surplus planes as well as trained pilots who wanted to continue flying. A former military pilot could pick up a Curtiss "Jenny" for a few hundred dollars. Many such aviators became barnstormers, performing aerial stunts at airports across the country and introducing local residents to flying at five dollars a ride. This was Las Vegas' introduction to aviation.

Late in 1919, aviation enthusiasts scraped out a dirt runway called Anderson Field just south of the city limits, on property many years later occupied by the Sahara Hotel parking lot. It was several months before the first plane arrived. Finally, in May 1920, former Army lieutenant Randall Henderson of Blythe, California flew in with his Jenny to give several prominent Las Vegans their first aerial view of the valley.

Anderson Field opened officially with an air show on Thanksgiving Day that same year. A tiny airplane named "Poison, Dose One Drop," was the featured performer. The pilot and designer was Clarence Prest of California. Poison lived up to its name when its 50-horsepower engine conked out at seventy-five feet. Someone had put castor oil into the gas tank instead of the crankcase. Prest survived the crash and briefly took up residence in Las Vegas, giving flying lessons to several of the town's elite. In 1922, he drew national attention by flying a new airplane from New York to Alaska. On the fuselage Prest had painted the plane's name and home base, "Polar Bear – Las Vegas, Nevada."

Biplane at Rockwell Field.

Western Air Express

One April morning in 1926, Western Air Express pilot Maury Graham arrived early at Vail Field near Los Angeles. He was decked out in the usual pilot's garb of coveralls, battered helmet, and goggles, and had a .45-caliber pistol strapped to his hip. He greeted his passengers, two Los Angeles businessmen, and settled himself into the rear cockpit of a World War I-era Douglas M-2 airplane. The passengers made do with seats up front atop the mail sacks.

Graham nosed the little biplane into the clouds and pointed it toward Salt Lake City. Cruising at speeds up to 115 miles per hour, the plane reached its refueling stop at Las Vegas' Rockwell Field, the former Anderson Field, in about three hours. The landing was a Las Vegas first for a scheduled air passenger flight. Flight instructions for the remainder of the flight were simple: stay to the right of the Union Pacific Railroad tracks to avoid colliding with the southbound flight.

Western Air express was one of the first twelve companies to be granted a civil airmail route by the United States Government in 1925.

It and its descendant company, Western Airlines, based their claim to being America's senior air carrier on this very early beginning in commercial aviation. Following a merger with Delta, the name and logo of Western Airlines disappeared from the Las Vegas scene. On that historic day in 1926, Western Airlines made Las Vegas one of the first cities in the nation to enter the modern world of scheduled airplane travel.

Rockwell Field served as Las Vegas' municipal airport for three years after service began in 1926. Owners didn't renew the lease and Western Air Express began shopping for a new field in 1929. As luck would have it, local businessman "Pop" Simon was building a new airport about eight miles northeast of the city. It was to be the terminal for Ne-

The first Western Air Express depot was located on what is now Paradise Road and Sahara Avenue.

vada Airlines, a new airline company. Nevada Airlines initiated there the first regular passenger service between Reno and Las Vegas, but even with the backing of world-famed speed pilot Roscoe Turner, only a few flights were ever made. Simon then negotiated a lease with Western Air Express. In November 1929, Western moved its operations northeast of town.

At about that time, the huge new 12-passenger Fokker tri-motor became the airline's main passenger airplane. The interior of the Fokker was luxurious and spacious compared to the cramped mail compartment of the old M-2, but there was a drawback. The light, predominantly wood airplane tended to bounce a bit in heavy weather. Though passengers were given "burp bags" and the plane's windows could be opened conveniently, it was sometimes necessary to hose out the cabin after a rough flight.

Western entered the 1930s as one of the nation's largest airlines. Then the federal government intervened to forge a national transcontinental network. In 1930, the U.S. Post Office Department forced Western into a partial merger with Transcontinental Air Transport. The new company, Transcontinental and Western Airlines, got the coveted airmail contract for the Los Angeles to New York route. Though Western did retain its original route through Las Vegas, most of its planes and personnel went to TWA. By 1934, the airline was back down to six pilots flying four airplanes.

This postcard was sent out to commemorate the first airmail service in Las Vegas, April 17, 1926.

McCarran Airports

In the mid-1930s, decreased federal airmail subsidies and general economic depression drove America's airlines to the brink of bankruptcy. Though the number of passengers through Las Vegas constantly grew, Western Air Express nearly vanished. After 1938, the situation improved.

The efforts of Senator Patrick A. McCarran of Nevada were crucial. On the national scene, McCarran sponsored the Civil Aeronautics Act of 1938 that created an independent aviation authority and provided reasonable regulation. He also pushed for federal appropriations for airport development.

McCarran remembered his home state as well. He was instrumental in the creation of a U.S. Army Air Forces gunnery school alongside commercial operations at the airport northeast of Las Vegas. The Army opened the base just as America went to war in 1941. McCarran also helped obtain federal funds that enabled the city to improve and light the runways and build a passenger terminal. The civilian facility was officially designated McCarran Field in honor of its benefactor. After World War II, the Air Force briefly closed its air base at McCarran. It was reactivated at the senator's urging in 1949 and renamed Nellis Air Force Base a year later.

Western Air Express, Las Vegas' pioneering airline, regained its vitality in the late 1930s. Creative marketing was a big factor. Western rerouted some of its daylight flights, allowing passengers a view of the spectacular scenery of Boulder Dam, Grand Canyon and Utah's national parks. Western also got into Las Vegas' burgeoning wedding business. Special "Honeymoon Trips to Paradise," appealed to California couples ducking that state's more

Western Air Express passengers deplaning.

The first McCarran Airport shared its field with the Las Vegas Army Gunnery School. Senator Pat McCarran is seen at the entrance.

restrictive marriage laws. For those in a real hurry, the airline arranged to have a minister perform the ceremony at the airport.

During World War II, the DC-3s of Western Airlines and TWA[2] shared the runways with B-17s of the Army Air Forces. That arrangement worked well enough given the wartime emergency, and the airlines continued to use the field after the air base was inactivated in 1946. The Air Force planned to reopen the base, but there was one major condition – commercial airlines would have to vacate. Led by Senator Pat McCarran, Congress added an additional inducement to build a new airport, dangling the prospect of large federal appropriations. Immediate action was crucial, but city and county governments dithered for the better part of 1946 over where to build the new field.

The first proposal, a new airport near Main Street and Las Vegas Boulevard, fell through when the owners refused to sell. The county then looked more seriously at an offer made by Las Vegan George Crockett. In 1942, Crockett had cleared three dirt runways south of town near the Los Angeles highway and added a hangar and tarpaper shack. Within a few years, tiny Alamo Airport had expanded into one of the premier general aviation facilities in the country.

By 1946, Alamo could handle any of the large commercial airplanes then in service. Crockett offered the airlines free use of his field for up to three years. While the county negotiated with Crockett,

voters overwhelmingly approved a $750,000 bond issue in May 1947. Construction on a new airport began the following January. On December 19, 1948, Senator McCarran attended a huge celebration dedicating the second airport to be named in his honor.

Bonanza Airlines

Through the first seventy years or so of Nevada's existence, the vast distance between northern and southern population centers was a formidable barrier to the political integration of the state. It wasn't until 1935 that Las Vegas-Tonopah and Reno Stage lines pioneered a bus route between Las Vegas and Reno. Regular air travel had to wait another decade for the end of World War II.[3]

In the summer of 1945, a small airplane charter service, Most and Bacon, began operations out of the tiny Skyhaven Airport north of town. A few months later, the company became Bonanza Air Service. Bonanza's two small Cessnas took tourists on scenic flights to Grand Canyon, Death Valley, and Hoover Dam. Press releases boasted that the customers included many of the celebrities then beginning to appear in Las Vegas showrooms. Bonanza's other enterprises were pilot training and ambulance service.

The influx of tourists that followed the war justified incorporation and the purchase of a surplus C-47 early in 1946. Decked out with flowered curtains and leather-upholstered seats for twenty passengers, it became a presentable civilian DC-3. The company used its new

flagship to inaugurate regular passenger service between Reno and Las Vegas in August 1946.

From the first, Bonanza sought a U.S. mail contract to offset losses on passenger operations. The company's salvation finally came in 1949 through a merger with Arizona Airways. By early January, passengers could fly from Tucson to Reno via Las Vegas. In 1968, the Bonanza logo disappeared into that of a merged Air West, but the airline will be remembered for its contribution to bringing Reno and Las Vegas closer together.

Chapter Notes

[1] Cactus Kate's was also, for many years, a casino beside Interstate 15 south of Las Vegas.

[2] For a few years after 1938, TWA (the airline was then known as Transcontinental and Western Airlines) also operated out of the small Boulder City airport. It kept a couple of DC-2s there to make the short hop to Las Vegas with connections to San Francisco.

[3] Nevada Airlines flew the route in 1929 but only for a few flights

Bonanza Airlines DC-3 and company officials, c1946.

Chapter THREE

Law and the Courts

The Bar of Justice

Occasional high-profile murder cases remind us that the law is frequently Byzantine in its processes and justice often a chimera. In early Las Vegas, justice might have been just as elusive, but court procedures were a good deal simpler and swifter. Take the fairly ordinary case in the early 1930s of a fatal shooting at the Double O bar and brothel in the red light district on First Street. The justice of the peace, functioning as coroner, summoned witnesses, lawyers, jurors and the defendant to the scene of the crime for the inquest. With a bung starter for a gavel, he presided from behind the bar.

Hardly had the proceedings begun when a motion for recess by the state permitted the district attorney to slake his thirst with bootleg whiskey. All present, including the defendant, participated in this unusual courtroom ritual. Several times during the questioning of wit-

The mementos here were gathered by collector Ron Donoho to honor Las Vegas law enforcement officers. At bottom is a badge once carried by Ernest May, the first Las Vegas city policeman killed in the line of duty. Badge at right belonged to Don Borax, chief in the 1940s, while the .32-20 Colt revolver at top belonged to Dave Mackey, chief in the late 1930s. The badge immediately below it is thought to have been Mackey's also.

Las Vegas Review-Journal

nesses, the bottle again made the rounds. While the defendant slept, the coroner prompted his jury with generous slugs of whiskey as they deliberated, if that is the right word

at that juncture. When the jury duly reported a verdict of self-defense, all approached the bar for consultation and a final round.

One side effect of the opening of a large air base near Las Vegas in December 1941 was pressure to close the city's red light district downtown. City attorney Paul Ralli made news that month for refusing, for lack of evidence, to prosecute twenty-one women residents of the area. His decision likely stemmed from his long experience in defending such cases. In a 1946 memoir, Ralli claims that as a private attorney, he never lost a case in municipal court. If, by some chance, the city judge was inclined to find a client guilty, Ralli would at once serve notice of his intent to appeal to district court for a jury trial. The infuriated judge, who then had to certify all the papers to the district court, invariably dismissed the case.

In justice court, Ralli's ploys were more sophisticated. Elected

JPs of the time were more likely to be businessmen or ranchers than attorneys. Often, they were overly impressed by legal complexities. In one typical case, the prosecutor confidently rested his case after producing three men who testified that they saw Ralli's client strike the aggrieved party. Ralli blithely produced six witnesses who swore that they did *not* see the blow. He then read, at considerable length, from numerous legal volumes to the effect that in the event of conflicting testimony the weight of evidence must be considered. The prosecutor didn't consider that such an argument merited the dignity of a reply. The judge, however, apologized to the dumbfounded district attorney, explaining that he had no recourse but to find the defendant not guilty. What these three cases have to do with justice is a moot point, but they surely present a more satisfying spectacle than many a more recent televised legal circus.

Six Companies versus Ed Krause

The two court trials of Boulder Dam construction worker Ed Krause in 1933 would have tested the journalistic skills of the most hardened Chicago crime reporter. Florence Lee Jones, fresh out of journalism school and employed by the *Review-Journal*, proved she was up to the task. Krause, a truck driver, had brought a civil suit against Six Companies, Incorporated, builders of the dam. He complained that carbon monoxide in the diversion tunnels had caused incapacitating dizziness and nausea. He also claimed that it ruined his sex life.

Threatened with a rash of such suits, Six Companies fought back ruthlessly. The industrial giant assigned a special undercover agent named John Moretti the task of proving Krause's disability claim fraudulent. Moretti took his job very seriously. Befriending Krause, he first involved the construction worker in the robbery of an old prospector and likely even instigated the crime. He also arranged a party for Krause and invited a pair of alluring women friends. Reporting later from the court room, Jones wrote that the young women's testimony about the specifics of the evening had the men straining to hear every word and the women hiding their faces in their hands. Testimony made it clear that Krause's sex life was not seriously impaired.

Six Companies lawyers, gloating over their successful impugning of Krause's character, were stunned when, after a six-week trial, the jury deadlocked. Another jury in the robbery trial immediately afterward voted for acquittal. Neither panel, it appears could stomach the tactics of Moretti and Six Companies. Krause's suit for damages was never retried, but the company later settled some fifty such cases out of court. Florence Jones, the young society editor, went on to a long a distinguished career in Las Vegas journalism.

The Blue Room

According to newsman John Cahlan, the Blue Room in Las Vegas was as notorious in its day as the infamous eighteenth-century prison known

---

[**1900**]　　　　　　　　[**1920**]　　　　　　　　[**1940**]

1908 FBI FOUNDED BY TEDDY ROOSEVELT

1920 WOMEN GET VOTING RIGHTS
PROHIBITION 1920—1933

1870
African-American men granted voting rights with passage of Fifteenth Amendment.

1881
Outlaw Billy the Kid shot dead by Sheriff Pat Garrett in New Mexico.

1890
Elizabeth Potts hanged for murder, the first and only woman to be executed in Nevada.

1905
Sam Gay, a bouncer at the Arizona Club, is hired in 1908 as Deputy Sheriff of Lincoln county.

1900
Edwin and William Kiel found murdered on the Kiel ranch.

1910
Sam Gay fired. Later Gay is elected Sheriff.

1911
Peter Buol elected first mayor of Las Vegas.

1914
Women get right to vote in Nevada.

1917
Sheriff Sam Gay fired.

1918
Sam Gay re-elected.

1920
Nineteenth Amendment grants right to vote to all American women.

1921
Dugan murder trial

1924
J. Edgar Hoover appointed head of FBI. Begins fighting crime, real and imaginary.

1925
Scopes "monkey trial" challenged law forbidding the teaching of evolution in Tennessee schools. (Scopes convicted of teaching evolution.)

1929
Al Capone's gang murders seven of George "Bugs" Moran's gang in Chicago Valentine's Day massacre. Moran escapes and dies in prison in 1957.

1932
Lindbergh baby kidnapped in N.J. The child is later found dead.

1933
Six Companies v. Ed Krause

to history as the "Black Hole of Calcutta." Built in 1911, the Blue Room on Second Street served as the county lockup until 1935, when the county swapped jails with the city. Designed to accommodate only twelve inmates, the main cell room measured a mere 16 x 28 feet. Conditions there had been a disgrace for years when the jail population reached a peak of 108 in 1943. No tears were shed in 1947 when the Blue Room was sold to make room for the expansion of the Apache Hotel, later Binion's Horseshoe.

The sale did provide the occasion for Cahlan to reminisce about some of the more colorful Blue Room occupants. Most prominent among these was "River Joe" Whitney, the most arrested man in Las Vegas. River Joe earned his nickname by being among the first workers at the Boulder Dam construction site on the Colorado River. Cahlan probably exaggerated only a little in claiming that Joe spent time in the jail on fifty separate occasions.

His first actual fame came in 1936. A visiting congressman from Washington State slipped Joe a few pints of whiskey while the latter was on a jail work gang. Joe smuggled the loot back to his fellow inmates with predictable consequences. When the deceit came to light, Joe was joined for a few hours by his former benefactor. Faced with a six-month sentence in faraway Carson City in 1938, he left a work detail and was never seen locally again. In a 1942 letter to Cahlan from Alaska, where he was laboring on the strategic Alcan Highway, Joe included fond regards to the chief of police. Probably Joe mourned the passing of the Blue Room just a little.

Sam Gay

Through its first quarter century, Las Vegas was basically a small town oriented to the railroad tracks and dependent upon the railroad payroll for its survival. If one had to choose the historical figure who most epitomized the town during this era, Sheriff Sam Gay would be a strong candidate. A large genial man with a penchant for good

whiskey, Gay was much beloved by the citizenry. This was due in large part to his frequent run-ins with the group he scornfully dismissed as "the courthouse ring."

In August 1929, Gay was tormenting the politicians again. District Attorney Harley Harmon was under pressure to do something about bootlegging and gambling. These two activities were still illegal, but a contemporary photograph in the *Las Vegas Age* showed patrons of the Northern Club on Fremont

Las Vegas Sheriff Sam Gay.

1934
John Dillinger gunned downed by FBI in Chicago.

Floyd "Baby face" Nelson found dead on road south of Chicago. Nelson had hidden out in Las Vegas prior to being killed.

1935
Bruno Hauptmann convicted in Lindbergh baby kidnap/murder case.

1946
Bridget Waters murder trial.

Ten Nazi war criminals are hanged after being convicted at the Nuremberg trials.

1963
President Kennedy assassinated.

1964
Civil Rights Act passed.

1966
Miranda case. Supreme Court rules that suspects must be "read their rights."

1970
Nixon makes Elvis an Honorary DEA Agent.

1971
Charles Manson convicted in the "Manson Family" murder of actress Sharon Tate.

1972
Five men arrested at the scene of a burglary in the Democratic National Committee's Watergate offices.

1974
Watergate hearings may lead to impeachment. President Nixon resigns.

1981
Regan appoints Sandra Day O'Connor; first woman Supreme Court Justice.

Justice O'Connor

1992
Three days of riots follow Rodney King verdict in L.A.

1993
Brady Bill passes. Requires waiting period, background checks, for handgun sales.

ATF attacks David Koresh at Waco. FBI takes over botched raid.

1995
O.J. Simpson acquitted of murdering estranged wife, Nicole, and Ronald Goldman.

Street lined up at what looked like a bar, and the men sitting around the tables were probably not playing Parcheesi. Harmon set Sheriff Gay on the trail of the gamblers. But Gay didn't dutifully break up the games at the Northern.

What he did do was breathtaking in its audacity. The Las Vegas Elks were then hosting their state convention. To provide a little amusement and help defray the convention costs, the lodge provided some games of chance. Sheriff Gay calmly walked in on the scene and closed up the games, announcing that he would permit no such lawbreaking activity. The incident left *Age* publisher Charles "Pop" Squires frothing with indignation. "Bravo Sam!" he editorialized. "Great Victory!" Presumably state Elks leader Harmon was none too happy either, though he wasn't one of the frustrated gamblers. Gay didn't lose his badge as he had over earlier affairs, but when he retired a year later, it was definitely the end of an era.

On August 24, 1932, Las Vegas mourned the passing of its much beloved former sheriff. Gay, a sometime rancher and later motorman with the San Diego Electric Railway, began his career as a lawman in 1905 as deputy to Sheriff Charles Corkhill. His first firing came in 1910 when Corkhill appointed a Democrat in his place. It was rumored that there was another reason for the firing.

Gay had chained county prisoners to a shady cottonwood tree beside Las Vegas Creek instead of confining them to the town's sweltering tin jail. For this humane gesture, it was said, Corkhill fired him even though a hundred local businessmen had signed a petition on his behalf. Later that year, Gay defeated his former boss in the election for sheriff.

Gay came close to being fired again in 1915. District Attorney Bert Henderson charged him, probably not without reason, with public intoxication. The County Commission chamber erupted with applause when Gay was retained after all, having solemnly promised never to take a drink so long as he wore a badge.

In 1917, Gay was again in hot water. His deputy, Joe Keate, took umbrage at a five-dollar contempt fine imposed for arriving tardily at the court of Justice of the Peace Bill Harkins. The deputy waved one pistol at Harkins, tossed another on the desk and offered to shoot it out. Instead of obeying Harkins's frantic order to arrest Keate, Gay calmed his deputy and led him from the courtroom. Gay was fired for nonfeasance, but the voters returned him triumphantly to office the next year. His judgment was sound, by the way, in the choice

Clark County Court House, Las Vegas, 1925.

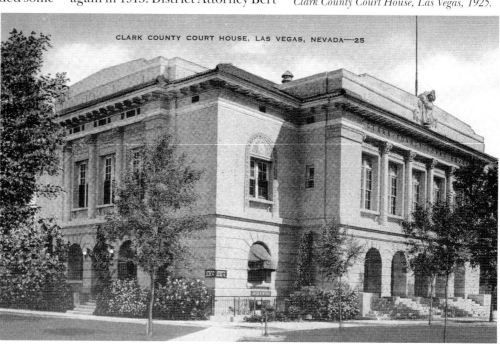

CLARK COUNTY COURT HOUSE, LAS VEGAS, NEVADA—25

of Harkins as an antagonist. His Honor, it seems went on to a long and illustrious career as a forger and jail breaker, gaining national renown as the "Houdini of Forgers." [But that's another story.]

The Dugan Trial

In late September 1921, the Clark County Commission announced the results of its drawing to determine district court jurors. There was nothing particularly remarkable about the list. It contained the names of fifty-five gentlemen from all walks of life. The problem was that the legislature of that year had forbidden the exclusion of any class of electors from the jury lists. This of course meant that women must be included. Members of the local bar grumbled openly — one claimed that a woman juror could not give a handsome man a fair trial — but the next list, for the January session of the court, included the names of twenty-two women.

The first case on the January docket was a fairly ordinary murder case. The testimony of several witnesses agreed that Nick Dugan had been partaking heavily of moonshine whiskey at a dive on Block 16. They also agreed that he fatally shot a patron of Lambert's Restaurant after an altercation. Dugan's lawyer argued only that his client, because of his condition, couldn't distinguish right from wrong.

Judge William Orr gave the jury five options ranging from first-degree murder to not guilty. All eyes were on the four women jurors, one of whom was Helen J. Stewart, already a forty-year Las Vegas resident. In the first ballot, the four women held out for second-degree murder against the men's insistence upon the lesser charge of involuntary manslaughter. After two more ballots, the twelve agreed on the lesser charge. The women had proved, at least in this first historic trial, that they could judge at least as harshly as men.

The Review-Journal *extensively covered the Bridget Waters trial in Las Vegas. The September 3, 1946 paper announced the murder charges.*

Bridget Waters

If the first women jurors served in Clark County as early as 1922, it took a good deal longer to seat the first black juror. He was Earnest Jeffries and the murder trial for which he was a juror was a doozy, drawing front-page treatment across the nation and in Europe.

It began as a divorce proceeding, not unusual in Las Vegas in the 1940s. But this one, involving a war bride, had an international twist. Frank Waters, a native Las Vegan working in Northern Ireland, had married an Irish lass in 1944. Waters was later transferred to France where he wrote to his wife Bridget that he was displeased with their marriage. Bridget heard no more from him until he filed for divorce in Las Vegas in October 1945.

In April of the following year, Bridget Waters arrived in Las Vegas with her infant son to contest the divorce. Newspapers and women's groups in Great Britain had urged her to bring a test case for the protection of deserted war brides. At the widely publicized trial, Waters claimed that Bridget had been unfaithful, but letters from him describing his own romantic adventures apparently led the jury to deny the divorce and grant custody of the child to Bridget.

The story might have ended there except that on Labor Day 1946, Frank Waters went to his wife's Las Vegas residence to pick up his son for an afternoon visit. An argument ensued and Bridget, claiming to fear for her son's safety, shot him through the heart with a .22 pistol. The case would involve the cream of the local legal profession.

On September 3, 1946, District Attorney V. Gray Gubler announced that he would press a first-degree murder charge against Bridget Waters. There was immediate international sympathy for the attractive young war bride. Local residents started a defense fund, as did an English village where Bridget had worked as a nursemaid. An avalanche of mail, mostly favorably inclined toward the accused, arrived at the city jail. One letter did cause her some distress. A woman denounced her, claiming that men were too scarce for her to go around killing them off.

Sensing a great sob story, John Cahlan of the *Review-Journal* and private investigator Bud Bodell attempted to interest famed Hollywood lawyer Jerry Geisler in the case. That arrangement fell through, but the threat led the D.A. to add former city attorney Paul Ralli to the prosecution team. Defense lawyer L.O. Hawkins responded by bringing in prominent local attorney Marion Earl. The family of the deceased hired a California press agent.

The trial began on October 21. A battery of American and foreign newsmen reported Bridget's claim that her husband had threatened to take their child. High points of the trial were the summations. With wild gestures and savage shouts, Ralli called the defense case a "shameless lie." Earl, in a brilliant and low-key response, reminded the jury of his friend Ralli's former career as a professional actor. The jury listened and brought in a verdict of involuntary manslaughter, the lightest possible charge. That evening, Bridget Waters dined with the British consul at a popular local nightspot. A few days later, she began what would be a three-year prison term in Carson City. And so ended what was, up to that time, Las Vegas' most notorious murder trial.

Gun Law

In mid-October 1953, a 20-year-old man, recently released from a Texas mental institution, began hanging around the bar at the Las Vegas Club on Fremont Street. He played the hit song "Crying in the Chapel" repeatedly on the jukebox and seemed particularly moonstruck by an attractive cocktail waitress. On one of those occasions, the waitress brushed him off. He quickly drew a pistol and fired twice, critically wounding her in the side and back. Two more shots fatally injured an unemployed bartender standing nearby. The pistol had been purchased at a local pawnshop.

Two months later, robbers waved guns at a clerk at Sue's Liquor Store on South Fifth Street and made off with $160 and a gold watch. On the same day, a onetime special officer with the sheriff's department, trying to stop a fight at a North Main Street garage, pulled a pistol from his pocket and fired two shots into the air.

This spate of gun-related incidents was too much for *Review-Journal* editor Al Cahlan. "What was he doing with the weapon in the first place?" Cahlan raged, referring to the last event. "The ease with which individuals manage to be carrying guns continues to shock average individuals." Then he got to the meat of his editorial comment. "Too often," he said, "possession of a gun in a crisis means that gun is going to be used, usually with tragic consequences." Cahlan had begun a one-man crusade for stricter gun laws. Within two weeks, he was editorializing again. The city commission, the grand jury and various Clark County officials had been debating a firearms sale control act for three months with no resolution. Gun dealers and sportsmen's associations had expressed opposition to a waiting period for the purchase of a pistol. Some, Cahlan said, even opposed any type of gun registration. Why hadn't any member of the general public spoken up in favor, he wanted to know. He urged the politicians to speak in their behalf and pass an ordinance.

In early February 1954, the city commission responded, passing by a vote of four to one, an ordinance forbidding the display of guns in shop windows and requiring that a person be of voting age to purchase one. The law went further; it provided for the registration of all concealable handguns. Rex Jarrett, the one commissioner voting against the measure, opposed it because it did not require a waiting period. The issues are as contemporary as yesterday's headlines.

Chapter FOUR

Vegas Vices

Prohibition

The New Year of 1919 dawned clear and dry — emphasis on the dry. In November, Nevada voters had gotten the jump on national prohibition and voted to ban the sale of liquor. Statewide, the vote

Teacups were used in speakeasy clubs to diguise the liquor in case of a raid.

was lopsided. With just 22,000 votes recorded, Dries outnumbered Wets by over 4,000. Clark County voted by more than two to one to ban alcohol. Only in Searchlight was the vote close; Bunkerville voters, on the other hand, went sixty-six to one in favor. New Year's Eve was a mournful affair for the state's Wet minority.

On January 4, 1919, newly re-elected Sheriff Sam Gay made a stern pronouncement: "I am going to enforce the prohibition law to the letter," he said. "Mr. Bootlegger, this is your first and last notice from me. Your next notice will be a warrant of arrest." In fact, arrests and prosecutions didn't begin in earnest for about a year. The initiative was so badly written that the legislature later had to specifically exempt such items as vanilla extract and perfume.

Prominent Las Vegan Lon Groesbeck bore the brunt of the first serious test of the law in January 1920. For the Salt Lake Brewing Company, Groesbeck had supervised the building of the Northern Club on Fremont Street in 1911. As he continued to purvey fine whiskey through 1919, the new law made him a criminal. Sheriff Gay, himself an unabashed toper, got a warrant and found twenty-three pints of Old McBrayer in Groesbeck's room at the Northern. Groesbeck's subsequent conviction by a jury in September finally ushered in the prohibition era in Las Vegas.

Liberty's Last Stand

In May 1931, R.A. Kelly found himself in an interesting new line of work. A former real estate agent, Kelly was now the proprietor of a new Las Vegas saloon called Liberty's Last Stand at 10 Stewart St. This wasn't so unusual in itself, but this was the Prohibition era, and Kelly was working for the U.S. Department of Justice. Federal agents had recruited him to play a central role in Las Vegas' first major "sting" operation. Illegal liquor sales at the saloon were recorded on hidden Dictaphones, and Kelly learned the locations of numerous local distilleries, breweries, and speakeasies.

Toward the end of May, Kelly abruptly sold Liberty's Last Stand and purchased a popular roadhouse on Boulder Highway. On the morning after the sale, bootleggers arrived in droves with their wares; there to arrest them were twenty armed agents. Simultaneously, thirty-five other agents raided virtually every establishment within an eight-mile radius and rounded up more than ninety suspects. Some official red faces did result, however, when it was later reported that a swarm of townsfolk had descended on a happily untended saloon and gleefully emptied beer barrels into handy tomato cans for transport home. News of the raid hit the front pages from coast to coast, but the affair of Liberty's Last Stand had little lasting impact in Las Vegas. The bootleggers of course soon reopened and thrived until the Twenty-First Amendment pretty much put them out of business two years later.

End of Prohibition

Times were bleak in early March 1933. A wave of bank closings, including many in Nevada, took the Great Depression to new depths. For some, there was one small ray of light. The newly inaugurated president, Franklin D. Roosevelt, had promised the end of Prohibition. The first announcement from Washington came on March 8. Federal prohibition agents would no longer seek prosecution of owners of speakeasies and rum joints.

Local bootleggers shrugged; it wouldn't make much difference, because there hadn't been much federal prohibition activity to speak of anyway. By the end of the month, Congress legalized the sale of beer of up to 3.2 percent alcohol content, effective April 7. Brewers reassured consumers that that was 3.2 percent by *weight*, that is, roughly comparable

to pre-Prohibition beer of about four percent by *volume*. Wine of a similar percentage was also allowed by the legislation, but California wine growers sneered that they would refuse to make "insipid slop" that no one would drink.

By the end of March, City Clerk Viola Burns was struggling to complete fifty-two applications for beer licenses. Distributors promised an adequate supply of Old Bohemian, Acme and Pabst Blue Ribbon by the fateful date, but there were some delays in receiving the brew. Shipments destined for Las Vegas were mysteriously diverted to larger markets. When the beer finally did arrive about 9 a.m. on April 8, there was a minor additional problem — there were few bartenders who remembered how to tap a keg.

There was no riotous celebration, but downtown streets as well as clubs along the highways were jammed until the wee hours. Police announced that they made no arrests for gross intoxication. The initial supply of tap beer was guzzled in about twenty-four hours, but it was OK. There was more where that came from.

Divorce Las Vegas Style

Early in the twentieth century, Reno took advantage of Nevada's short residency and lenient laws to earn the title "Divorce Capital of the World." In 1920, screen star Mary Pickford's divorce in nearby Minden caused something of a scandal and helped create a new

industry for the Silver State. Commentator Walter Winchell called it "RENO-vation."

Las Vegas began skimming off some of the divorce business in the mid-1930s. Among others, Tarzan creator Edgar Rice Burroughs and Evangeline Stokowski, wife of the renowned symphony conductor, chose Las Vegas over Reno as a place to "take the cure." The big break for the bumptious Southern Nevada town came in 1939. Maria Gable arrived in January and by pre-arrangement moved into a Seventh Street house vacated by her attorney, Frank McNamee, Jr. Maria, usually called Ria, had been separated from husband Clark Gable for two years, and it was an open secret that Clark wanted a divorce in order to marry Carol Lombard.

Ria expected, she said, to spend the next six weeks catching up on her knitting, but she didn't count on the eagerness of the Las Vegas

press to boost the city in the aftermath of Boulder Dam's completion. Still, she came to enjoy the attention and played along with the

Ria Gable (standing) plays roulette at the Apache Club while waiting for a divorce from Clark Gable in 1939.

publicity campaign built around her stay in Las Vegas. Photos and newspaper reports went out over the wire services. Ria was shown skiing at Mt. Charleston, boating at Lake Mead, and playing number 35 on the Apache Club's roulette wheel. A brief proceeding in the chambers of Judge William Orr on March 7, 1939 ended the eighteen-year marriage. Clark soon married Carole and, with a big boost from Ria, Las Vegas soon overtook Reno as the world's divorce capital.

Mr. Gormley's Divorce Problems

On the surface, there was nothing unusual in the February 1920 divorce in Minden, Nevada of screen star Mary Pickford from husband Owen Moore. What was extraordinary was the fact that Mrs. Moore had been a Nevada resident for exactly sixteen days, whereas Nevada law called for a residency period of six months. Yet the divorce was perfectly legal. A deliberate quirk in the state's divorce law permitted the waiving of the residency requirement if the defendant just happened to be "found" in the county. Owen, quite "coincidentally" showed up in Minden. Divorce granted. The state's Attorney General ranted and raved but could do nothing about it.

At about the same time, another Californian, James Gormley, tried to work the same ploy in Las Vegas. Gormley and his wife Ramona had traveled together to Las Ve-gas, whereupon the erstwhile Mrs. Gormley, having been "found" in the county, was immediately served with divorce papers. Judge William Orr granted the divorce routinely. James returned to Los Angeles where he married a wealthy heiress two days later.

There was one problem. According to Mrs. Gormley's testimony, later heard by Judge Orr, James hadn't informed his wife of the real nature of their business in Nevada. Mrs. Gormley apparently was led to believe that she was in Las Vegas to sign papers relating to a mining deal. She claimed that the divorce had been obtained by fraud and perjury. The sympathetic judge overturned the divorce decree. The District Attorney immediately sought charges of perjury against Gormley and had him extradited to Las Vegas. At a preliminary hearing in March, defense attorneys argued that it didn't matter whether Gormley had told the truth or not because the entire case had been voided by the decree overturning the divorce.

Meanwhile, James Gormley still had two wives. This small problem seems to have been resolved by the lucrative settlement of an alienation of affections suit brought by wife number one against wife number two. That freed wife number one to sue James for divorce. When the perjury trial finally came up in October, no one really cared any more. After five days of testimony, the jury threw up its hands and freed the defendant. Getting a quick divorce in Nevada was not always as easy as it was cracked up to be.

"Ma" and "Whataman"– A Case Study

In 1931, Nevada shortened its residency requirement as a spur to the divorce trade. Reno already had a reputation as a divorce colony; Las Vegas got a start on one that year with the notoriety attending the tangled affair of Minnie Kennedy and Guy Edward Hudson.

In July, national headlines screamed Hudson's nickname, "Whataman." Whataman Hudson had fled Los Angeles after posting bail on a bigamy charge. This was not extraordinary in itself, but it cast doubt on the status of his three-week-old marriage to Minnie Kennedy. Minnie, better known as "Ma" Kennedy, was a well-known southern California evangelist. She was also the mother of the more famous evangelist, Aimee Semple McPherson.

The Kennedy-Hudson marriage was quickly annulled. Whataman came to Las Vegas, ostensibly to sell Buicks for Jim Cashman, but actually to dissolve his first marriage. Ma followed him to Las Vegas and took the town by storm, preaching a hellfire sermon atop a blackjack table at Fremont Street's Boulder Club. On August 18, Whataman had his divorce and the loving couple was united in a ceremony on a cliff overlooking the Boulder Dam construction site. Accompaniment was provided by workmen exploding dynamite in the canyon below.

Sad to say, the perfect marriage didn't take; it ended just a year later amid public acrimony. Whataman went on to put together a nightclub act in Colorado where he billed

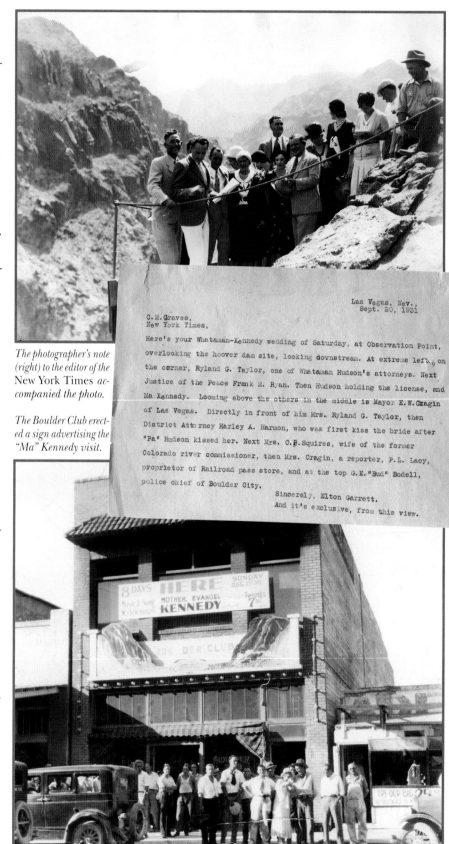

The photographer's note (right) to the editor of the New York Times accompanied the photo.

The Boulder Club erected a sign advertising the "Ma" Kennedy visit.

Las Vegas, Nev.,
Sept. 20, 1931

C.M.Graves,
New York Times,

Here's your Whataman-Kennedy wedding of Saturday, at Observation Point, overlooking the hoover dam site, looking downstream. At extreme left, on the corner, Ryland G. Taylor, one of Whataman Hudson's attorneys. Next Justice of the Peace Frank M. Ryan. Then Hudson holding the license, and Ma Kennedy. Looming above the others in the middle is Mayor E.W. Cragin of Las Vegas. Directly in front of him Mrs. Ryland G. Taylor, then District Attorney Harley A. Harmon, who was first kiss the bride after "Pa" Hudson kissed her. Next Mrs. C.P. Squires, wife of the former Colorado river commissioner, then Mrs. Cragin, a reporter, P.L. Lacy, proprietor of Railroad pass store, and at the top G.E. "Bud" Bodell, police chief of Boulder City.

Sincerely, Elton Garrett.
And it's exclusive, from this view.

himself as a "sexologist." After a brief career in show business, he returned to obscurity. Las Vegas would host many more celebrity divorces and marriages, but few could match the circus qualities of the affair of Ma Kennedy and Whataman Hudson.

Dude Ranches

W.E. Alexander was just a little ahead of his time. In 1936 he leased Lorenzi's Lake Resort northwest of town and announced that he was turning it into a dude ranch. His idea was to encourage prospective divorcees to spend the required six-week residency in Las Vegas instead of Reno. The million-dollar scheme didn't materialize but, as Twin Lakes Lodge, Lorenzi's Resort did eventually become a divorcees' retreat in the 1940s.

Meanwhile, the Las Vegas divorce of Ria Gable from movie star husband Clark Gable in 1939 created an rush of imitators. Mr. and Mrs. E.L. Losee of New York seized the opportunity and purchased the Kiel Ranch in North Las Vegas. This ranch, developed by Conrad Kiel in the 1870s, was, after the Las Vegas Ranch, the oldest in the valley. The Losees converted several ranch buildings, including the 1911 mansion of Las Vegas banker John S. Park, into guest rooms, and built additional accommodations. Renamed "Boulderado," the resort operated successfully for a number of years. In 1940, Universal Studios featured the Boulderado in a movie, further boosting the fortunes of Southern Nevada.

Lorenzi Lake Park in the 1930s.

In recent years, the old Boulderado has seen evil times. Most of the outbuildings crumbled before finally being demolished by the City of North Las Vegas, and the Park mansion was razed by fire some years ago. Until recently, the only extensive piece of real estate in Las Vegas Valley where one could see evidences of more than a hundred years of history, the property is now much diminished by development and has but two remaining structures.

The Boulderado's stiffest competition for the divorce trade came after 1946. Rodeo champion and long-time western movie star Hoot Gibson opened the D-4-C just west of the developing Las Vegas Strip. With its own airstrip, clubhouse and rodeo arena, the D-4-C catered to an exclusive clientele. With these and several other ranches operat-ing by the early 1950s, Las Vegas easily captured from Reno the title of Nevada's divorce capital.

Marriage

In June 1940, Las Vegas set a new one-day record: a hundred and four marriage licenses granted. That made nearly four thousand since the beginning of the year, twice the number for the same period in 1939 and three times that of 1938. Las Vegas boost-ers gleefully calculated that this was more than one wedding per capita over the course of a year, higher than Reno's rate.

Through the 1930s, Las Vegas had conceded to Reno the title of "Divorce Capital of the World," but the southern city had begun to develop a flourishing wedding trade. The presence of such newly married celebrities as Clara Bow,

William Boyd, Lew Ayres, Edgar Rice Burroughs, Fred MacMurray, and Bela Lugosi lent considerable glamour to the little town near Hoover Dam.

Probably, it was the highly publicized marriage of singer/movie star Nelson Eddy in January 1939 that loosed an avalanche of weddings in Las Vegas. That, and the passage late that year of a law in California requiring medical certificates before marriage. Coming as it did on top of the mandatory three-day "gin marriage" waiting period in that state, the new California law made Nevada marriages seem a lot more convenient. Wedding chapels began to proliferate along Fifth Street.

At about the same time, Las Vegas began to overtake Reno in numbers of divorces granted as well. The town then happily played the role of Hollywood's Gretna Green for the stars who came to get divorced and immediately remarried — those for whom, in Samuel Johnson's phrase, "hope triumphs over experience."

The Hitching Post Wedding Chapel on a rare snow day in Las Vegas in the 1950s.

The Keno Battles of the '30s

The origins of Chinese lottery, or "white pigeon ticket," are shrouded in the mists of ancient Chinese history. Its modern form, the game of keno presented a special set of problems, even after the state legislature legalized gambling in 1931. This is because Article IV of the state constitution flatly prohibits lotteries.

Keno was a particularly vexing problem in Las Vegas in the 1930s. As it was played until then, the game more closely resembled modern bingo; players filled numbers on their cards with dried peas as up to ninety numbered balls were drawn from the "goose neck." The game continued until there was a winner. The winning player then received all the money wagered, minus a percentage for the house. The city

---

PROHIBITION 1920—1933

POST-WAR BABY BOOM

1901
Carrie Nation begins campaign to close saloons and ban alcohol by smashing kegs of booze in Topeka, Kansas.

1905
Las Vegas founders set aside Blocks 16 and 17 as the tavern district.

1909
First marriage certificate filed in Clark County.

1918
Nevada enacts statewide Prohibition.

1920
National Prohibition law enacted.

1930
Pair-O-Dice Club opens as the first nightclub on The Strip. It closed and reopened several times because it offered both gambling and liquor sales, before either was legal.

1931
Las Vegas bootleg sting shuts down speakeasy bars, temporarily.

Nevada legalizes gambling.

The Meadows Country Club resort opens.

1933
Prohibition ends.

1935
Alcoholic Anonymous founded.

1939
Easy divorce laws make Nevada a mecca for divorce seekers.

The Pair-O-Dice Club sold to Guy McAfee who renames it the 91 Club.

80-ball, "racehorse keno" made legal in Las Vegas.

1940
Clark County issues 4,000 marriage licenses. Three times the number of previous year.

1941
Block 16 "red light" district shut down.

El Rancho resort opens, has first Las Vegas buffet.

1950
Senate Committee on Organized Crime opens hearings on illegal gambling. Many gamblers go west to be "legal."

1951
Lili St. Cyr accused of "lewdness" for her striptease act performed at the El Rancho.

1955
Gaming Control Board created.

commission preferred not to view this form of keno as a lottery.

There the matter might have rested, but in January 1932, the Northern Club on Fremont Street was running an eighty-ball variant of the game. In this version, the player marked his own card and was paid at a flat rate if his numbers came up. To city judge William Orr, this looked suspiciously like a Chinese lottery. He upheld the city commission's denial of a license to the Northern Club. Against hopes to the contrary, a new city commission in 1933 was similarly ill disposed toward the game.

In 1934, hard economics swayed the city fathers where the arguments of the club owners had failed. The county commission granted a license for eighty-ball keno at the Tower Club in North Las Vegas. Though it looked as if that game was opened to force the issue on Las Vegas, the Las Vegas city commission feared the competition from the north. They knuckled under, giving tentative approval to the popular game.

There were more reversals over the next five years. In 1939, the eighty-ball game resurfaced as "racehorse keno." As in present day keno, players marked their own cards, and many games could be played without a winner. Northern Club operators argued that this game was played in every other city in Nevada. Despite the fact that District Attorney Roland Wiley had opined that the game was an illegal lottery, the city commission granted a license for racehorse keno to the Northern Club. The game duly opened and no one seems to have raised the issue of its constitutionality since.

Tony Cornero and The Meadows

Several men have been accorded the title of "father of the Las Vegas resort industry," but "Bugsy" Siegel usually gets the nod. However, there are still a few old-timers around who would vote for the little-remembered Tony Cornero. It was Cornero who opened what was arguably the first luxury resort in Las Vegas in 1931.

The Meadows was just beyond the city limits on the new Boulder Highway and conveniently outside Las Vegas police jurisdiction. The Meadows was by far the swankiest nightclub in the small town, and the location on the heavily traveled route was perfect. The owners were old hands at importing fine whiskey, a useful background in those days of prohibition. Tony, in fact, wasn't able to join his brothers, Frankie and Louie, for the grand opening, being at the time a guest of the

Tony Cornero in 1955.

1966 MINI SKIRTS ARE IN FASHION 1972 WATERGATE   1999 CLINTON IMPEACHMENT HEARINGS

1957
First meeting of Gamblers Anonymous held in Los Angeles.

On December 29, El Rancho hosts the weddings of Eydie Gorme and Steve Lawrence and Paul Newman and Joanne Woodward. (Both couples are still married.)

1948
McDonald's revolutionizes the fast food industry. Its

assembly-line "Speedy Service System" serves customers in less than a minute. Ray Kroc takes it nationwide in 1955.

1957
First bare breasts revealed in Minsky's burlesque show at the Dunes.

1960
FDA approves the birth control pill and the sexual

revolution kicks into high gear.

1964
The surgeon general first warns that smoking causes cancer.

1973
Linda Lovelace stars in X-rated film, *Deep Throat*. She later testifies to Congress about the evils of the porn industry.

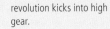

1993
200,000 people gather on The Strip to watch the imploding of the Dunes.

1995
Gaming Control Board reports 176,995 slot

machines and 5,782 live table games statewide.

The Fremont Street Experience opens downtown.

2000
Americans spends more on fast food than on higher education.

2003
Indian casinos nationwide employ more people than in Nevada casinos.

2004
Gaming revenue on Indian reservations in California alone is expected to surpass all of Nevada's by 2010.

Pop singer Britney Spears weds Jason Alexander in Las Vegas. The marriage is annulled 55 hours later.

The Meadows Country Club in 1931. Below, the Meadows after the fire that destroyed it.

Their timing was no better. Work on Hoover Dam was largely completed and Las Vegas was dwindling. Even with a scantily clad chorus line, it was the last hurrah for the Meadows. It operated only intermittently until it was destroyed by fire in 1943.

It was far from Tony Cornero's last hurrah. For a time in the late '30s, he operated a gambling barge, the *S.S. Rex*, off the California coast until federal agents dumped his slot machines overboard. Undeterred, he reopened the *Rex* at the corner of Second and Fremont in Las Vegas, where the Horseshoe was to follow a few years later.

Tony Cornero didn't live to see his crowning achievement; he died while watching a craps game at the Desert Inn just about a month before his Stardust Hotel and Casino opened across the street.

Guy McAfee and the Californians

In retrospect, 1939 can be seen as a critical milestone in the development of Las Vegas. Since the legalization of gambling in 1931, the city had feared for its reputation and downplayed its vices. Fremont Street casinos — the Northern, the Apache, the Boulder Club and the Las Vegas Club — were very low-key. It took events in distant Los Angeles to bring about the active promotion of gambling.

In February 1939, Los Angeles police raided several illegal Sunset Strip gambling establishments. News reports indicated that there were numerous film stars present. The raids were part of a series car-

federal government at McNeil's Island for rum running.

One thing the brothers didn't have was timing. Apparently, the Corneros thought they had a deal with city politicians. Block 16, the downtown red light district, would be forced to close, and the entire operation could be moved out to the Meadows. If they had a deal, it fell through with the election of new officials in 1932. Block 16 stayed open for another decade. Also, thinking that they would

have a special dispensation where Nevada's anti-gambling laws were concerned, the Corneros were stunned when the state legislature threw gambling wide open just after they started construction. They essentially bailed out of actual operation of the club in 1932.

The resort became a popular nightspot for locals, but it was never a huge success. In 1935, new owners remodeled it after a famous Los Angeles nightspot and opened it as the Meadows Cocoanut Grove.

The Pioneer Club at First and Fremont in the 1940s. Below, Guy McAfee.

ried out by the city's new reform administration. Gambling house operators began looking for a more congenial environment.

Among the first was Guy McAfee, a former police vice captain turned gambler. Moving to Las Vegas, McAfee opened the Frontier Club on Fremont Street. Soon afterward, he converted the Pair-O-Dice Club on the Los Angeles Highway into the 91 Club. It was, in fact, McAfee who claimed credit for nicknaming that stretch of highway the "Strip." His patrons from Hollywood's film colony began making regular appearances at the tables.

McAfee was followed by others. In 1942, Tutor Scherer and others opened the Pioneer Club at First and Fremont. At about the same time, two transplanted New York-

ers, Ben Siegel and Moe Sedway, arrived from California to open a racehorse-betting parlor. What these men imported from California to Las Vegas was vitally important — gambling expertise, large bank-

rolls, and their movie star patrons. If Los Angeles officials hadn't cracked down on gambling, what might Las Vegas have become?

Senator Kefauver Looks Down His Nose

Proposals emanating from Washington for something like a National Commission on Gambling periodically throw a bright spotlight on Nevada's major industry. Certainly not for the first time. In 1950, the U.S. Senate created a committee to investigate organized crime in American life. Estes Kefauver of Tennessee, its chairman, saw himself as a staunch upholder of traditional values and an implacable foe of gambling in any of its forms. This wasn't uncommon. Most of the rest of the country looked at Las

Vegas with loathing. It's also pertinent to note that Kefauver harbored presidential ambitions; a series of nationally televised hearings could catapult him into the White House.

On November 15, 1950, Kefauver and two other committee members blew into Las Vegas and conducted a marathon nine-hour hearing. Their intent, Kefauver told the press, was to investigate information that some Nevada casino operators were part of a national crime syndicate.

Only a few gamblers and public officials were interrogated. Most of the nuggets of information they heard could have been gleaned from any passerby on Stewart Street: Moe Sedway had operated race wires in Las Vegas since 1942, and Wilbur Clark was only a minority partner in the Desert Inn. Before vanishing later that day, committee members expressed their outrage. "I think it's about time somebody got damn mad and told these people where to get off," Senator Charles Tobey sputtered. Senator Alexander Wiley added that "public morality has sunk to a new low." According to them, the state's licensing sys-

Senator Estes Kefauver of Tennessee.

tem served only to give gangsters a cloak of respectability.

Local commentators were a good deal more blasé; the hearing was a publicity stunt revealing little that was not common knowledge. They adopted the view later expressed by Robbins Cahill, the man then in charge of the state's

gaming control effort. Gamblers could not be expected to be bishops of the church or pillars of the community.

If this were the case, why then was the Kefauver Committee so fateful for Las Vegas? Because the hearings cast Las Vegas in such a bad light. The creation of the Gaming Control Board five years later was an important step in fending off crippling legislation from Washington and permitting Nevada's major industry to flourish.

Las Vegas' Most Notorious Block

Clark's Las Vegas Town Site became a reality at the auction of May 15, 1905. Temperance-minded railroad officials inserted a special clause into the deed of sale for lots in each of the forty square blocks — a clause forbidding the sale of liquor. In

each of the blocks, that is, except two: Blocks 16 and 17.

Within days of the auction, saloons clustered in Block 16 along the east side of north First Street between Ogden and Stewart. Entrepreneurs in ritzier sections of the tent town spotted a loophole in the deeds: liquor could be sold in hotels and rooming houses elsewhere in the town site. Bars basically indistinguishable from those on Block 16 grew up along the first block of Fremont Street. A few beds upstairs made them *look* like hotels. But the die was cast — Block 16 became Las Vegas' tavern district. The Block shortly achieved further notoriety as the city's red light district, with fifty or so "working girls" in more or less permanent residence.

All of this came to a screeching halt in December 1941. The commander of the new Army Air Corps Gunnery School northeast of town threatened to declare all of Las Vegas off limits unless city officials did something about the red light district. Fearing the economic consequences, the city acted. In the wee hours of December 2, most of the police force conducted a raid described in the local press as "serio-comic," and Police Commissioner Tinch announced "the place is shut down." The "girls" were soon back in business, of course — this time on Boulder Highway — but the notorious Block 16 was history.

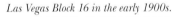

Las Vegas Block 16 in the early 1900s.

The Media

Al Cahlan

Journalists like Charles "Pop" Squires and the Cahlans — Al, John and Florence — are important sources for the history of Southern Nevada. They were also community leaders in their own right.

Albert Edmunds Cahlan, for example, was in the thick of many significant political battles of the 1930s. Cahlan came to Las Vegas in 1926 to manage the *Clark County Review*, an ancestor of the present *Review-Journal*. While his younger brother John handled most of the straight news reporting, Al devoted himself to his influential column, "From Where I Sit," and to his first love, politics. He quickly gravitated toward the center of the community power structure and its most important figure, Ed Clark.

The fiercest political fight of the mid-1930s concerned the issue of a municipally owned power company. Supporters of the idea rallied around Mayor Leonard

People counting votes at the Review-Journal *office after the 1945 election included Berkley Bunker (standing left), Florence Lee Jones Cahlan (center), Al Cahlan (second from right), and Frank Garside (right).*

Arnett. Opponents were led by Clark, who also happened to head the power company. The quarrel reached a peak when Arnett allegedly dropped Cahlan to the street with a solid right to the chin. The episode ended with Arnett's abrupt resignation amid rumors that he had been bought off.

Cahlan seemed to lose interest in politics after 1940 when he was

not appointed to fill out the term of deceased U.S. Senator Key Pittman, an appointment he thought he had locked up. A vicious editorial duel with rival publisher Hank Greenspun of the *Las Vegas Sun* sustained him through the 1950s. He resigned from the paper in 1960, but his column continued to appear for several years before his death in 1968.

Woman in the Dunes

The tabloids regularly make startling announcements about politicians meeting aliens from outer space or about finding Noah's lost ark. One suspects a certain disregard for the canons of responsible journalism here. But creating news, as opposed to reporting it, has a history as old as the Gutenberg press.

Certainly it has a hallowed tradition in Nevada. Mark Twain and Dan DeQuille, reporters for Virginia City's *Territorial Enterprise,* were excellent journalists, but they were not above inventing stories on slow news days. The man who froze to death in mid-summer in Death Valley and the thousand-year-old petrified man created international interest in the 1860s. Most of the jokes were harmless, but even Twain crossed the line when he reported that a well-known resident of Empire City, had slain his wife and nine children. Readers didn't think about an unstated clue that the public leg was being pulled: the subject was famously a bachelor, who therefore had no such family to murder.

Las Vegas journalists have not proved immune to this kind of tomfoolery. The late John Cahlan of the *Review-Journal* left a candid memoir about how he occasionally created stories or, in more modern parlance, "managed" the news. One story of the early 1940s that played nationally for weeks was a publicity stunt cooked up in conjunction with the filming of the movie *The Lady Eve.* In cahoots with the publicity department of Paramount Studios, Cahlan reported sightings of a

Florence Lee Jones Cahlan in 1963, when she resumed writing the Review-Journal's *"Socially Speaking" column.*

young woman cavorting nude in the dunes of, appropriately, Paradise Valley.

The plan was that the studio would supposedly locate the young woman and give her a screen test and an important role alongside Barbara Stanwyk and Henry Fonda. Paramount would, of course, bring in a Hollywood starlet at the appropriate moment. Successive reports penned by Cahlan embellished the story: the mysterious young woman was foreign-born and perhaps suicidal. Her plight generated national interest, and

Sheriff Glen Jones, who was in on the plot, received calls from as far away as England.

At what was to be the dramatic *coup de theatre,* Paramount's legal department reneged on the deal and Cahlan was left holding the bag. Real events then took a turn straight out of de Maupassant. A young divorcee confessed to the sheriff that she had enjoyed assignations in the desert with her attorney and was afraid she had been found out. Cahlan blithely sent out this true story of a woman in the dunes, thus sating the national appetite for a satisfying conclusion and saving the newspaper's reputation for probity.

Florence Lee Jones

Florence Lee Jones Cahlan had many firsts to her credit; she was a founding member of the Junior League of Las Vegas and the first woman member of the Junior Chamber of Commerce. She was also Las Vegas' first woman journalist.

Fresh out of journalism school in 1933, Florence Lee Jones took a job as cub reporter on the *Review-Journal*, then expanding at the peak of Boulder Dam construction activity. Her colleagues were managing editor Al Cahlan and his brother John, whom she would later marry. As the only woman on a small town newspaper, she was automatically dubbed "society editor," a title she later dismissed as a sham and a fraud.

Her first outing as society editor in fact turned into a small disaster. After an evening of prowling the city's many nightspots, she wrote the first in what was to be a series of columns on the people she saw, what they were wearing and the places she visited. The nightclub owners were delighted, and sales skyrocketed at local dress shops. One prominent churchwoman, however, wasn't thrilled at having been spotted at the wrong place. The threat of withdrawn advertising ended the column after just one appearance. Jones soon got her chance at a front-page story and proved herself a capable journalist.[1]

Florence Lee Jones interviewing actor Francis Lederer in 1937.

The *Las Vegas News*

Early in 1940, the *Las Vegas Review-Journal* announced that Bill Busick had been added to its advertising staff. Many years later, *Review-Journal* newsman John Cahlan recalled the hiring as a very bad move. "You could tell by his conversation," said Cahlan, "that he was leaning toward communism." Busick was fired after only a year.

In January 1941, at the height of the turmoil between two city commissions, Busick began publishing the *Las Vegas News*. His first editorial column explained his firing as a result of asking too many questions — questions about shady deals between prominent local businessmen and the politicians who were blocking the reform efforts of Mayor John Russell.

A week later, Las Vegas' newest newspaper publisher was blasted as a communist and subversive at an "Americanism Week" rally at the War Memorial Building. The speaker, one Larry Doyle, claimed to have seen Busick speaking in Glendale, California with a hammer and sickle in one hand and a portrait of Joseph Stalin in the other. The story got heavy play from Busick's former employers.

In subsequent issues of the *News*, Busick explained that he had long been a labor organizer and editor of labor journals, but a fervently anti-communist one. Certainly his newspaper, while fiercely defending Mayor Russell and alleging official corruption, showed no Stalinist tendencies. Issues of the *Las Vegas News* continued to appear until mid-May when the commissioners deposed Russell. On May 26, 1941 mortician Howell Garrison was appointed mayor. This eliminated the *News*'s main reason for being and ended this curious episode in Las Vegas' journalistic history.

The Free Presses

For most of the early years of Las Vegas, residents enjoyed the benefits of a newspaper rivalry between the Republican *Las Vegas Age* and the Democratic *Las Vegas Review*. In 1929, the *Review* absorbed a short-lived rival to become the *Review-Journal*, and in 1934, dwindling subscriptions forced the *Age* to cut back to weekly publication. Except for having to beat back a challenge from the *Tribune* in the mid-1940s, the *Review-Journal* reigned alone over the small world of Las Vegas journalism for the next sixteen years.

The *Las Vegas Free Press*, an upstart of 1950, proved unexpectedly difficult to dispose of. The *Free Press* arose out of a strike by the International Typographical Union against the *Review-Journal*. As they had done in similar circumstances in other communities, the typographers established their own paper, a tri-weekly, in competition with the struck newspaper. Volume I number 1 of the *Free Press* came out on May 3, 1950. Its front-page editorial spoke of "honest, fair and unafraid" journalism but made no direct reference to the immediate cause for the paper's origin. Nor did it acknowledge its union ownership. There was virtually no local news, except for a front-page report of the defeat of the Las Vegas Wranglers by Tijuana in a Sunset League baseball game. Merely a strike weapon against the *Review-Journal*, the *Free Press* was clearly no match for its established competition.

Not at least until Hank Greenspun entered the picture. At that time in charge of publicity for the new Desert Inn Hotel and Casino, Greenspun broke ranks with other resorts by placing a small ad in the *Free Press*. He also angered his boss, Desert Inn owner Moe Dalitz. Greenspun suspected that the *Review-Journal* had squawked to powerful Nevada Senator Patrick McCarran, an important protector of Nevada gambling and a man whose causes the *Review-Journal* had long championed.

It was only the opening round. Within three months, Greenspun purchased the bare bones *Free Press* plant on north Main Street, changed the paper's name, and began publishing the *Las Vegas Sun*. His front-page column "Where I Stand," a take-off on the rival editor's "From Where I Sit," immediately began zestfully blasting the *Review-Journal* and its hero, Pat McCarran. Las Vegans were again treated to a lively press duel that continues to the present under successor editors.

The *Las Vegas Free Press* reflected a major concern of a generation of Americans — communism. Its first issue took note of, and lamented, the defeat in the Florida primary of Senator Claude Pepper, an ardent supporter of President Truman. Truman's opponent, Representative George Smathers, had charged that Pepper was pro-communist and a backer of Truman's program of "socialized medicine." The paper carefully proffered its own anti-communist credentials, pointing out that managing editor Henry Moscow had helped rid the Newspaper Guild in New York of communists and communist sympathizers.

The name *Las Vegas Free Press* was revived in an entirely new newspaper twenty years later. Its first issue, published on New Year's Day 1970, demonstrated seismic changes in social concerns in the interim. On the front page, editor and publisher Jay Tell proclaimed the Age of Aquarius. "Let your hair down, loosen up brothers and sisters," he told his readers. "Life is short and every moment feeling guilty about joy and love is a moment wasted." While avowing abhorrence of violence and revolution, Tell committed the newspaper to total freedom of expression, the exposing of corruption, the puncturing of stuffed shirts and the calm presentation of liberal and radical ideas.

Instead of traditional reliance on UPI and AP press reports, the *Free Press* subscribed to the Underground Press Syndicate and Liberation News Service. It was clearly aimed at a younger readership. A two-page center spread was devoted to a debate on the legalization of marijuana. District Attorney George Franklin argued vociferously against the notion. The paper's more sympathetic reception of the idea perhaps gives a clue to the prominent placement of ads offering the services of bail bondsmen. Few of the other advertisements were of mainstream commercial establishments; most hawked posters, incense candles, headbands, acid lights and strobes. A concerned Sheriff Ralph Lamb wrote to inquire if the *Free Press* was patterned after an underground paper of the same name in Los Angeles. He was assured that the paper did not advocate the breaking of any laws.

As editor, Tell himself later noted, the '60s were over. Underground newspapers either went mainstream or folded. The *Free Press* folded in the fall of 1971.

Las Vegas' First Radio Station

Listening to radio in Las Vegas was a very difficult proposition before 1940. For one thing, there was no local station. In the evening, Las Vegas listeners could pick up broadcasts from Los Angeles and Denver, but apparently inexplicable local static made the programs all but unlistenable. Most people seemed to blame the problem on power transmission lines, but the city electrician attributed it to cheap electrical motors which powered fans in most Las Vegas homes. Mayor John Russell thought streetlights were to blame and accused the electrician of not carrying a static detector while replacing street lamps.

John Heaton was to change all that, if only for a short time. A railroad man, he came to Las Vegas in 1905 and served as railroad agent for twenty-five years. Nearing retirement in 1929, he began to devote himself to a new dream — creating the first radio station in Las Vegas.

Working with a Los Angeles firm, he announced grand plans for offices on Fremont Street and network hookups. After several months of financial problems, his station, KGIX, was finally ready to go on the air from a modest studio on the outskirts of town. In February 1930, Las Vegans heard their first local radio programs, a series of test broadcasts between midnight and 8:00 a.m. Every night that week was billed as "Frolic Night" on KGIX. Gassy politicians divided up the airtime with local amateur and professional musicians.

Amid threats of bankruptcy over unpaid bills, regular broadcasting began in September. Programs were simple and short. Musical groups from nightspots like Lorenzi's Lake Resort or the Blue Heaven on Boulder Highway performed between 7:30 and 8:30. After that, there might be piano solos by Maydelle Pistole or the tenor voice of railroad electrician J.F. Cory. Records filled the remaining time until sign-off at 9:30. An hour and a half of daytime programming included "Home Hints" by Mrs. A.E. Hensler, news and weather by John Cahlan, and more records.

A sheriff's sale ended the dream the next year, though even then Heaton tried to reopen the station as the "Voice of Boulder City." When he died in 1937, the newspapers barely mentioned KGIX, saying that it operated as long as advertising revenues permitted. Somehow, it's not a bad epitaph.

FM Radio

Frequency modulation arrived in Las Vegas on November 30, 1961. That's frequency modulation as in FM radio. FM is a bit of electromagnetic wizardry that enables radio waves to carry high fidelity sound.

[**1700**]　　　　　　[**1800**]　　　　　　[**1900**]

100BC 1st Bound Book in China　　1715 Typewriter invented, England　　1792 U.S. Postal Act　　1815 3,000 P.O.s in U.S.　　1900 Kodak Brownie Camera　1926 Book-of-
1650 1st Daily Newspaper, Germany　　1791 1st Amendment Passed　　1860 Pony Express　　1911 1st Airmail　Month Club St

1455
Gutenberg prints Bible. By 1500 half a million printed books were in use.

1754
Ben Franklin publishes first political cartoon in an American newspaper: a severed snake, represents the Colonies, titled "Join, or Die."

1791
The First Amendment is ratified by States.

1841
Horace Greeley first publishes the *New York Tribune*.

1844
Samuel Morse (right) sends first inter-city telegraph message.

An operator demonstrates the printing telegraph in 1908.

1854
Nevada's first newspaper, the *Gold-Canon Switch* is founded in the mining camp Johntown.

1862
Unsuccessful as a miner, Samuel Clemens (Mark Twain) begins writing and editing for the *Territorial Enterprise* in Virginia City, Nev.

1876
Alexander Graham Bell invents the telephone.

Mark Twain publishes novel, *The Adventures of Tom Sawyer*.

1901
Radio era is born when Guglielmo Marconi receives the first wireless signal across the Atlantic.

1903
The Vitagraph Theater, the first movie house in Nevada, opens in Reno.

1917
First Pulitzer Prizes awarded.

1922
First radio station in state, KDZK, established in Reno.

1930
First radio station in Las Vegas, KGIX, goes on air.

1936
Life magazine is first published by Henry Luce.

It was Donald W. Reynolds and his Southwestern Broadcasting Company that made FM programming available for the first time to Las Vegas radio audiences. Or at least to that handful of people who had FM radios. According to Reynolds, his local station, KORK-FM, was only the second station in the country designed from the beginning to broadcast in stereo.

FM sound quality was far superior to AM, but the programming was even more dramatically different. The first FM musical selection heard in Las Vegas was Franz Josef Haydn's Symphony No. 53, as played by the Vienna Symphony Orchestra. Symphonies, chamber music and jazz trumped the top-twenty tunes and daytime soap operas of AM radio. The station featured complete operas two evenings a week. It also promised that commercials would be fewer and more tasteful, and that musical pieces would not be interrupted.

To help parents cope with the new technology, the newspaper coached them on how to trick teenagers into listening to classical music.

For those young people who thought Tchaikovsky "icky," they were to be reminded that the popular song "Tonight We Love" was lifted from that "long-haired Russian." It's an interesting twist of history that we now listen to that long-haired Russian from the Donald W. Reynolds Broadcast Center at KNPR-FM.

Television

Nineteen fifty-three was a big year for Las Vegas. Population growth was phenomenal, as evidenced by the fact that the names of 1,500 new subscribers were added to that year's telephone directory. The year was also notable for the first appearance of television in town. In March 1953, the Federal Communications Commission granted a permit for KLAS radio to begin building a television station on the grounds of the Desert Inn Hotel. It also issued a license to operate over Channel 8, one of three channels allocated to Southern Nevada. The new station would be a network affiliate of CBS, ABC and the DuMont Television Networks.

KLAS kicked things off in true Las Vegas fashion with a "Tel-O-Rama" celebration at the War Memorial Building. The weeklong exhibit and demonstration provided an opportunity for thousands of Las Vegans to see how television worked and to compare the picture quality of a dozen or more brand name sets. Telecasts from the War Memorial stage didn't carry very far, extending only to TV sets on the floor of the auditorium.

But the programming during that week was undoubtedly more edifying than much of today's soap opera and quiz show fare. Students of the music and drama departments of Las Vegas High School performed, as did young dancers from the Jeanne Roberts School of Dancing. Nellis Air Force Base presented musical comedy, and Howard Capps, golf pro at the Desert Inn, gave golfing demonstrations. In anticipa-

---

1927 NBC, CBS | 1934 Drive-In Movies, N.J. | 1948 Transistor Invented | 1959 Microchip Invented | 1969 Live Photos | 1972 HBO Launches | 1985 Cell Phones in Cars | 1996 Movies on DVD
Radio Broadcasts | 1934 FCC created | | | sent from the Moon | Pay Per View | | 1994 U.S. Privatizes Internet

1938
October 30, CBS radio broadcasts Orson Welles' radio play *War of the Worlds*, inciting hysteria in New York.

1939
Gone With The Wind and *The Wizard of Oz* premiere in Hollywood.

1944
Computers like Harvard's Mark I put into public service. The age of

information science begins.

1946
Cannes, France holds its first International Film Festival. The scheduled debut in 1939 was postponed due to Hitler's invasion of Poland.

1947
The World Series is first broadcast on TV. By 1959, 90 percent of homes in the U.S. get a television.

1948
The *Chicago Tribune* scoops everyone with incorrect headline: Dewey Defeats Truman.

Transistor invented, enabling the miniaturization of electronic devices.

1969
ARPANET, the first Internet, is started.

1971
The Pentagon Papers on Vietnam appear in the *NY Times* and *Washington Post*.

1972
The *Washington Post* begins reporting on the Watergate burglaries. Other papers largely ingnore the story until it becomes a huge scandal, forcing President Nixon to resign in 1974.

Life magazine ceases publication, citing overwhelming competition from other kinds of media.

1979
First cellular phone communication network goes live in Japan.

1983
Time magazine names the computer as "Man of the Year."

First cellular phone network started in the U.S.

1994
American government releases control of Internet and WWW is born.

2000
DVD movie sales exceed one million per week.

tion, Las Vegans rushed to such outlets as Oran Gragson's North Main Furniture Store to buy their choice of Admiral, Emerson or Crosley sets.

Actual broadcasting began two months later. On the evening of July 22, 1953, Governor Charles Russell threw the switch and Las Vegans saw their first local TV. Chet Lauck and Norris Goff, "Lum and Abner" of radio fame, acted as emcees for the event, interviewing an array of TV stars including Gail Storm, Herb Shriner, and George Jessel. Regular programming, which started the next day, was a bit anti-climactic: three hours of test pattern, news from 6:00 to 6:10, five minutes of sports, two short films and sign-off at 10:10.

It was a year and a half before KLAS Channel 8 had any competition. The call letters of the second station, KLRJ, identified its prime mover, the *Las Vegas Review-Journal* newspaper. The *Review-Journal* had been owned since 1949 by the Southwestern Publishing Company, headed by Don Reynolds. Within months of entering the Southern Nevada newspaper market, Reynolds had announced that his company would be the first to bring television to Las Vegans.

In fact, KLRJ was the second station, and even then its application met with some controversy. Channel 2, which was one of two channels still available for licensing, had been allocated to the city of Henderson. KLAS owners complained that KLRJ's broadcasting facilities on Boulder Highway were located suspiciously closer to Las Vegas

than to the city they purported to serve. The *Review-Journal* shrugged off the objection; it was natural, they said, coming as it did from Hank Greenspun, publisher of the *Las Vegas Sun* and a major KLAS stockholder. The Federal Communications Commission rejected the complaint as well, and KLRJ made plans to begin broadcasting by the end of 1954.

A delay in the delivery of equipment prevented the televising of that year's Rose Bowl game, but the station was set to kick off by the end of January 1955. At first, Eastern advertisers were dubious about the Las Vegas market. There were approximately the required 50,000 people in the viewing area, but it was very unlikely that there were the necessary 20,000 sets. Still, NBC-affiliated KLRJ did manage a more exciting line-up than Las Vegans were used to. KLAS had been mostly airing old movies interspersed with such heart-stoppers as "Looking at Cooking," "Feminine Views," and professional wrestling.

KLRJ signed on with a full-length performance of the opera "Tosca" from New York and followed that up with such programs as *Hit Parade*, *Dragnet*, *Meet the Press*, and the Friday night fights. The *Mighty Morphin' Power Rangers* wouldn't show up for nearly forty years, but young viewers could already thrill to the adventures of *Commander Lee and his Vegas Village Space Rangers*.

The Las Vegas News Bureau

Russian novelist Fyodor Dostoevsky was referring to St. Petersburg with its profusion of ornate palaces and

churches when he observed that some cities are more "intentional" than others. In the early twenty-first century, we might be tempted to point to Las Vegas as the most intentional of cities.

The post-World War II development of Las Vegas into a resort metropolis of glittering gambling palaces wasn't a natural evolution. The idea of Las Vegas was in large measure the inspiration of dedicated publicists. None of these were more significant than the talented photographers of the Las Vegas News Bureau. It was they who created the idea of Las Vegas and implanted it in the American imagination.

Systematic and well-financed publicizing of Las Vegas began in 1945. High-powered public relations firms managed the campaigns. In 1947 alone, 50 million readers were exposed to stories, advertisements, and photographs emanating from Las Vegas. The experienced firm of Steve Hannegan and Associates took over the account in 1948. It was Hannegan who created the News Bureau, originally called the Desert Sea News Bureau.

The ploys devised by News Bureau photographers such as Don English, Jerry Abbott and Milt Palmer were inspired. Cheesecake, often tied to the flimsiest of contrived events, was one device. Newspaper editors across the country eagerly printed News Bureau photos of beautiful dancers decked out in hardhat and tool belt during Na-

Three photographers of the Las Vegas news bureau — Don English, Milt Palmer, and Jerry Abbott — pose under the welcome sign.

tional Electricians Week or dealing cards to fat gobblers at Thanksgiving. The photographers usually set aside Monday mornings for creating "hometowns." These were photos of attractive tourist couples frolicking poolside that appeared as if by coincidence in the couple's hometown newspaper. Invariably, others took the bait and made their pilgrimages to Las Vegas.

Stunt photos such as the one showing tennis great Jack Kramer balancing a model on his racket or the "floating crap game" in the swimming pool at the Sands created an aura of pure fantasy. For avid readers of movie magazines, there was a deluge of celebrity photographs — Marlene Dietrich's famous see-through gown, Jimmy Durante clowning with Harry Truman, Zsa Zsa Gabor sporting an eye patch to hide a shiner. These made Las Vegas seem a better place than Hollywood for stargazing. It may not be going too far to suggest that the News Bureau conjured up a magical "Entertainment Capital of the World" before it existed in reality.

Chapter Notes

[1] See the trials of Ed Krause, page 38.

Chapter SIX

Education and Culture

Las Vegas School

Early September traditionally marks the end of summer and, for school children, a return to the schoolhouse. Not so in Las Vegas in the year of its founding. In September 1905, kids got a reprieve — there was no schoolhouse. The primitive tent structure by Las Vegas Creek, used as a school in the spring, had been converted to a courthouse and, in mid-summer, the school fund contained the grand sum of $25.10. Even in those tent-city days, this was hardly enough to build a school.

School superintendent Ben Sanders promised to have a building ready by fall, but Labor Day passed with no solution to the problem. Finally, in mid-September, the school board purchased the old Salt Lake Hotel for $150 and moved it out in the middle of nowhere at Second and Lewis Streets. School opened at last on October 2 with sixty-four pupils and two teachers. It's worth noting that the teachers had been required to take state-mandated certification examinations at Pioche, the county seat. There appears to have been no outcry from the teachers. The school board again ran out of money by March 1906, and the school year ended early.

The simple two-room wood frame building served well enough for five years. A fine belfry was added in 1910, just before the building burned to the ground in October. Classes met for a time at the Methodist Church, but an imposing new grammar school on Fourth Street was almost ready for occupation, and would stand for many years, until it was razed to build the Foley Federal Building. Six years later, the population had so expanded that a high school was added to the block just south of the new school. That building served as Las Vegas High School until 1930 and then housed the upper grades of the grammar school until it too burned in 1934.

A new Fifth Street School, built on the site in 1936, is still in use for city offices. Considering its Depression-era construction date, the building is a remarkable example of Spanish-Revival architecture. With its high ceilings, French doors to the outside in every classroom, and cool, open courtyards, it put much modern school architecture to shame. Its significance to the community was recognized in 1986 when it was added to the National Register of Historic Places.

School Bonds

As almost everyone knows, the Clark County School District has been struggling for years to keep up with explosive growth in the numbers of school-age children. Regularly, voters are asked to approve bond issues for school construction. From 1907 to 1955, Nevada's education system was rickety at best. The state provided only thirty percent of school funding for the two hundred or so school districts around the state. With local financing making up the difference, there were great disparities among districts. Some of the smaller school districts in Clark County faced great funding difficulties, but the Las Vegas district was able to do quite well by its school children. A substantial 1911 grammar school was supplemented in 1917 by a high school and in the 1920s by a bond issue-financed Westside grammar school for the lower grades.

The perpetual school crisis began in the late 1920s with the influx of new residents anticipating Hoover Dam construction. In 1929, Las Vegas principal and school superintendent Maude Frazier spearheaded a successful drive for a $350,000 bond issue to provide for a new 500-student high school. Las Vegas High School was filled to capacity almost from the first. An emergency just a few years later led to another bond vote, as the old

high school, then used as a junior high school, burned to the ground in 1934. Together with a grant from the New Deal federal program, the Works Progress Administration, that bond issue made possible the beautiful "Fifth Street School" on Las Vegas Boulevard.

With the completion of that school in 1936 and population growth leveling off after the dam was finished, Las Vegas school administrators relaxed. Then came the explosive growth of the war years. During the years 1941 to 1945, the Las Vegas School District jerrybuilt several wood-frame temporary schools as well as the new Mayfair and North Ninth Street Schools. The end of the war offered no relief to overcrowding. Paraphrasing a former television personality, school officials hadn't seen nuthin' yet.

The head of the local school board warns of overcrowding in the public schools. Over the last five years, he says, school attendance has increased seventy-eight percent

— thirteen percent in the last year alone. He goes on to suggest that even if the population growth ceased and all of the planned school buildings were ready for occupation on Monday, they would be completely filled. Passage of a large bond issue is absolutely necessary. Sound like today's news? Actually, the school board president was Dr. J.D. Smith and the year was 1946.

During World War II, Las Vegas had built several new permanent and temporary schools and added to existing facilities, but the temporary John S. Park School in the new Huntridge development was completely unusable, and a new building was desperately needed in that area. Over half a million dollars, allotted for elementary school construction, would permit enlarging several schools to the full eight grades. Nearly one million dollars would go to the expansion of Las Vegas High School, providing an

The old Las Vegas school building on Fourth Street was destroyed by fire in 1934. The elementary school is in the foreground and the high school is in the background.

Students of Las Vegas High School are seen in costumes, possibly for a school play, in the 1930s.

auditorium, a shop building and a new classroom facility. In a front-page editorial, the *Review-Journal* urged the voters to approve the bond issue.

At the end of April 1946, ninety percent of the voters agreed. By the end of the decade, almost all of the projects were completed. The new John S. Park School opened in 1948 and Frazier Hall at the high school was dedicated two years later. The building was certainly appropriately named.

Was the crisis over? Not by a long shot. Yet another bond issue was proposed in 1951. Mayor Ernie Cragin warned that Clark County's tax structure would be completely destroyed by the $2 million proposal. Though it took over two years, Las Vegas voters rejected the warning and passed the bond issue.

By then it was clear that the state system for funding education was completely inadequate. In the mid-1950s, Governor Charles Russell and the state legislature finally adopted a state sales tax and revamped the organization of education. A key person in those developments was Assemblywoman Maude Frazier of Clark County.

The Library

With the rapid population growth in Clark County, the opening of new libraries has become, if not quite routine, at least a fairly regular occurrence. The creation of Las Vegas' first library on the other hand was a very big community event. The Mesquite Club, a women's service organization, made a library campaign one of its priorities after the club formed in 1911.

It was 1914 before a suitable building became available. That turned out to be what was already known as "the old courthouse," built just five years earlier when Clark County had been carved from Lincoln County. The plain one-story concrete block structure on the public square had just been vacated in favor of a noble new permanent courthouse on the same block. The ladies of the Mesquite Club successfully applied for permission to use the structure for a library. A school holiday was declared and school children aided in cleaning up the premises for their new use.

It was fully a year and a half before library operations could begin and another year before the Club held a formal opening with a musical and literary program. Through 1917, the library was featured regularly on the front pages of the newspaper. The title and authors of all the new books, ranging from novels by Robert Louis Stevenson and Nathaniel Hawthorne to the Cyclopedia of Engineering, were listed. Most of them were donated.

During June of that year, the library was well patronized, with 204 books of fiction and 13 non-fiction volumes circulating. After a year of operation there were more than four hundred library cards issued, reflecting about twenty percent of the population. The library was so strapped that a fee of ten cents was levied for the first ten times a new book was checked out. For several years, the practice of listing new books in the newspaper continued. A modern reader can be forgiven a bit of yearning for a time when the literary tastes of the community were front-page news.

An historical marker placed there in 1980 by the City's Diamond Jubilee Committee recalls another fact about the old courthouse building. Until 1942, when the city took over the War Memorial Building where the city complex is today, the building also served as city hall. Some people might also lament the passing of a time when half of a tiny building could accommodate most of the functions of city government.

University of Nevada Looks South

The 1864 Nevada Constitution called for the creation of a state university, but not until 1872 did legislators take concrete action. That year, they solicited offers of donated land. Among the cities eager to comply were Reno and Carson City. Surprisingly, the legislature overlooked these metropolises and instead selected distant Elko as the site for a state university. The fact that governor "Broadhorns" Bradley hailed from Elko County undoubtedly had something to do with the selection.

The University of Nevada duly opened its doors at Elko in the fall of 1874 to seven students. Several years later, the student body reached its maximum size of thirty-five; it was clear that the Elko site was a failure. Bowing to the inevitable, the legislature moved the university to Reno where the first class enrolled in 1886.

Through the first half of the last century, Reno remained the state's major population center. But by 1950, Las Vegas began to challenge Reno's dominance. Wartime industry and military bases had tripled the southern city's population during the 1940s. One sign of Las Vegas' new stature came in early September 1951. University of Nevada English Professor James R.

Dickinson arrived in Las Vegas to arrange for extension classes. With two part-time instructors, Dickinson began teaching thirty students at Las Vegas High School. These were the first students at what eventually grew into the University of Nevada, Las Vegas. Until the opening of the Lied Library, Dickinson's name was commemorated in the James R. Dickinson Library on UNLV's campus. It's still remembered in a related architectural feature — Dickinson Library Plaza.

Movie Theaters

When the Redrock Theater opened on West Charleston in 1966, it was just another movie theater. When it went to five screens seven years later, it established a milestone of sorts — the area's first multiplex movie theater. Its closing[1] prompts a look back, way back, to the beginning of moving pictures in Las Vegas.

Ground was cleared for Las Vegas' first movie theater on the date usually regarded as the city's birth date, May 15, 1905. It was at

The interior of the El Portal Theater.

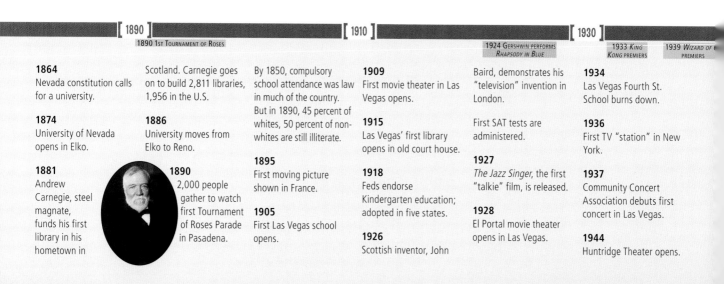

[**1890**]   [**1910**]   [**1930**]

1890 1ST TOURNAMENT OF ROSES

1924 GERSHWIN PERFORMS *RHAPSODY IN BLUE*

1933 *KING KONG* PREMIERS   1939 *WIZARD OF (* PREMIERS

1864
Nevada constitution calls for a university.

1874
University of Nevada opens in Elko.

1881
Andrew Carnegie, steel magnate, funds his first library in his hometown in

Scotland. Carnegie goes on to build 2,811 libraries, 1,956 in the U.S.

1886
University moves from Elko to Reno.

1890
2,000 people gather to watch first Tournament of Roses Parade in Pasadena.

By 1850, compulsory school attendance was law in much of the country. But in 1890, 45 percent of whites, 50 percent of non-whites are still illiterate.

1895
First moving picture shown in France.

1905
First Las Vegas school opens.

1909
First movie theater in Las Vegas opens.

1915
Las Vegas' first library opens in old court house.

1918
Feds endorse Kindergarten education; adopted in five states.

1926
Scottish inventor, John

Baird, demonstrates his "television" invention in London.

First SAT tests are administered.

1927
The Jazz Singer, the first "talkie" film, is released.

1928
El Portal movie theater opens in Las Vegas.

1934
Las Vegas Fourth St. School burns down.

1936
First TV "station" in New York.

1937
Community Concert Association debuts first concert in Las Vegas.

1944
Huntridge Theater opens.

1946
It's a Wonderful Life with Jimmy Stewart is released.

1948
First television network news broadcast.

1953
Department of Health Education and Welfare created.

1954
Brown v. Board of Education, Supreme

Court decision ends government-sanctioned school segregation.

1955
Nevada adopts state sales tax to pay for public schools.

Flamboyant pianist, Liberace, opens at the new Riviera Hotel.

1957
Classes begin at Nevada Southern University (UNLV).

1959
The "Rat Pack" friends, Frank Sinatra, Joey Bishop, Dean Martin, Sammy Davis Jr., and Peter Lawford appear together at the Sands.

1963
Betty Friedan publishes *The Feminine Mystique* and the women's movement is born.

A young Elvis performs Jail House Rock.

1969
Elvis opens his comeback show at the International.

500,000 gather in Woodstock, N.Y. for rock concert.

1974
A federal judge imposes forced busing of students to intergrate public schools. Riots ensue and trouble erupts in schools nationwide as the practice is adopted elsewhere.

2001
The Guggenheim Museum opens at the Venetian. A collection of 19th- and 20th-century artworks is displayed along with traveling contempory exhibits.

2004
The artworks of Claude Monet and other impressionist painters are displayed at the Bellagio's new art "museum."

Clark and Fourth Street. That's *not* Clark and Fourth Street downtown. The present-day site would be at the corner of Bonanza and "D" Streets in what's sometimes referred to as the old Westside. According to its builder, Chauncey Pulsipher, the 500-seat Trocadero Theater would be the equivalent of anything in New York. Unfortunately, the Westside began its precipitate decline that very day, as the new railroad town site east of the tracks sucked the life out of the older community. No Jujubes or popcorn for the edifice that remained uncompleted. According to early resident Charles Squires, the Trocadero Theater was a "monument to misdirected enterprise."

The next attempt apparently wasn't any more successful. In early 1909 the proprietor of the resort at the old Las Vegas Ranch announced that a dance pavilion and movie theater was in the works. Dances there became a regular feature of Las Vegas social life, but there's no indication that anyone ever watched movies beside Las Vegas Creek. Las Vegas finally got moving pictures later in 1909 with the Isis Theater, a little building snuggled next to the Opera House on Fremont Street near First. It was not magnificent, but it was a bargain. For twenty cents, one could see an hour's worth of one-reelers, including such blockbusters as *Dear Old Grandma, Monkey Stuff,* and *Too Much Snuff.*

The Isis Theater too was a short-lived operation. In 1911, that cracker box was razed to permit an addition to the original Las Vegas Club.

Theater manager James Squires didn't have far to look for a place to reopen. He acquired the old Opera House next door and converted it into the Majestic Theater. Belying its name, the former Opera House was not a place to catch Giacomo Puccini's latest masterpiece. There were some theatrical performances in the hall. *Mr. Savage,* billed as a beautiful society drama, was featured during a grand opening in 1908. But mostly the Opera house was used by local lodges and fraternal groups and for public meetings. Under later owners, Ernie Cragin and Bill Pike, the Majestic was Las Vegas' principal movie theater until the late 1920s.

On June 21, 1928, Cragin and Pike presented Las Vegas with a magnificent new movie palace, El Portal. For the grand opening, Paramount-Famous-Lasky Studios presented the world premiere of *Ladies of the Mob,* a tragic drama starring Clara Bow. Over 800 people purchased reserve seat tickets and admired the balconied Spanish windows and heavy chandeliers. After speeches by studio executives and Hollywood stars, Melodie Stone attacked the new Wurlitzer pipe organ to provide dramatic accompaniment to the action on the screen. After the grand opening, Las Vegans could see a new film every night with such stars as Gary Cooper, Greta Garbo and Lon Chaney.

The El Portal Theater, converted to non-theatrical commercial uses, still stands on Fremont Street between Third and Fourth. Well-maintained, it looks quite a bit as it did in 1928 though it hasn't

seen a star-struck movie crowd in a long time. Take a look at it anyway and imagine it as it was when talkies were about to change the way Americans lived.

Community Concert Association

The Southern Nevada Community Concert Association was part of the cultural life of Las Vegas for many, many years. The idea of creating the organization arose in the fall of 1936. A meeting the following January at the Apache Hotel's fashionable Kiva Club gave birth to the Las Vegas Co-operative Concert Association. The Association president, Waldo Taylor, was a local voice teacher and his four vice-presidents were musicians as well.

Dentist William S. Park was also an amateur thespian and organizer of theatrical performances. In the '1920s, he was known for presenting open-air concerts on his Zono-phone, an "improved Gramophone" talking machine. Lewis Rowe was a long-time art teacher and director of music and art at Las Vegas High School, and Mesdames Marion B. Earl and Roscoe Thomas played the piano and violin respectively.

Even though the community was dwindling in 1937 because of the completion of Boulder Dam, Las Vegans responded enthusiastically. By March, over six hundred people had subscribed, nearly ten percent of the population. Their fees of three dollars each permitted a concert season of three performances. On November 5, 1937, Helen Old-heim, a young mezzo soprano with the Metropolitan Opera, arrived

An art class paints in the Union Pacific Park between the depot and Main Street in the 1960s.

in Las Vegas for the first concert. After a luncheon hosted by Mrs. Artemis Ham among others, she enthralled a large audience at the new War Memorial auditorium with selections by Purcell, Brahms and Saint-Saëns.

In the remaining season, a Russian violinist performed the Mendelssohn Violin Concerto, and the program by American baritone Wilbur Evans explored lieder, opera, spirituals and vaudeville. It was an auspicious first season. Even the dark war years of the early 1940s did not halt the concerts, and the postwar period saw such luminaries as pianist Jorge Bolet and the world-famous Trapp Family of *Sound of Music* fame.

While carefully nurturing its rustic Old West image, Las Vegas did not neglect high culture.

Las Vegas Little Theater

On a good weekend, a Las Vegas theatergoer these days might be able to see three different plays, each produced by a different theater company. In March 1938, the only choice was *Hay Fever*. The Noel Coward comedy was presented by the newly organized Las Vegas Community Players. *Hay Fever* was the second of three plays in that first season of Las Vegas' first theater group.

For a small Depression era town, the company had a surprising abun-

dance of experience. Bob Woodruff had worked with the Cleveland Playhouse, Richard Fletcher with stock companies in Florida and Jack Beville with Grauman's Chinese Theater in Hollywood. English teacher Guild Gray had acting experience in college, while the group's president, lawyer Paul Ralli, had appeared onstage opposite Mae West in *Diamond Lil*.

In the Community Players' second season, a thriller entitled *Double Door* was added to the usual comedic fare, and in 1939, the company scored a success with the first of several annual performances of *The Drunkard* during Helldorado Week. Jack Beville had returned to Hollywood to study the revival of that nineteenth-century melodrama.

By 1942, the company had reorganized itself as the Little Theater of Las Vegas. That was the year of the group's crowning achievement to date. The play was Maxwell Anderson's *Eve of Saint Mark*, and many of the cast were soldiers from the Las Vegas Army Gunnery School. The fact that some of the soldiers would soon be overseas added poignancy to the occasion. The war itself curtailed theatrical activities in Las Vegas, but the Little Theater was reorganized and going strong again in 1946.

Chapter Notes

[1] Redrock Theaters closed in 1999. The property was demolished in 2002.

Chapter SEVEN

Sports

Annual Rodeos

The annual spectacle of the World Championship Rodeo in Las Vegas each December provides an occasion to look back at the growth of the sport in what was not so long ago a small Western village. In December 1927, Las Vegas' first annual New Year's Rodeo was in the planning stages. Actually, civic memory was a little short; it was really Las Vegas' *second* First Annual Rodeo.

The *first* First Annual Rodeo was held at the new downtown fairgrounds in January 1923. The Union Pacific Railroad had just donated to the city property on the north side of Stewart Street. At that event, more than a thousand spectators, close to half of the town's population, watched a hundred cowboys compete. A world championship-caliber cowboy named Brassfield walked off with first prizes in saddle-bronc and bareback riding and shared the prize in steer riding with two others. The affair was a financial success

Rodeo events were a fixture at Helldorado.

— the Rodeo Association netted a hundred dollars and the sponsoring American Legion $183.

The 1927 rodeo was a much bigger event. Prizes of up to two hundred dollars were awarded in horse racing, calf roping, goat roping, bronc riding and bulldogging. The Union Pacific and Grammar School bands added to the festivities. The event was decidedly underreported by the local press. The *Las Vegas Age* chose to focus on a mule that had experienced the rodeo's only near-death experience. The beast had clamped its teeth into cowboy Joe Rogers's hand and refused to open wide. The cowboy was about to use a pistol to end the confrontation when a friend impressed the mule and saved its life by applying a lighted cigar to its nose.

The next annual Las Vegas rodeo, staged at Lorenzi's Lake Resort, didn't occur until seven years later. Not until 1936, with the addition of a rodeo to the second Helldorado celebration, did the rodeo really did become an annual tradition in Las Vegas.

Henry Wilson and the Las Vegas Desert Rats/Tigers/Giants

When Henry L. Wilson died in May 1944, his brief obituary said only that he was a well-known pioneer black resident of Las Vegas and had worked for several years in the city's sewer department. The article didn't elaborate on why he was well known.

He was probably the same Henry Wilson who organized and managed Las Vegas' first black baseball

Possibly the first organized baseball team in Las Vegas.

team. In July 1925, Henry Wilson got together a group of black ballplayers and challenged the Santa Fe Giants of Needles, California. He managed his Las Vegas Tigers to an 11-9 victory a week later. The game initiated ten seasons of successful black baseball in Las Vegas. Though the team changed managers several times and was known variously as the Desert Rats and finally the Giants, Henry Wilson was always there in the infield.

In 1930, the Tigers might have had a claim of sorts to the city championship. They were eight-and-one going into the final game with the Union Pacific Athletic Club, a team they had already beaten twice. It was something of a grudge match since the Tigers had won the previous game on a forfeit. The UP team had left the field on a disputed call by umpire Gene Ward. The UP won that last outing 7-6, due in part to a spectacular play by

catcher Bill Hall. Hall threw out a base runner at home despite being severely gashed in a collision with a parked car.

Henry Wilson was a leader off the field as well as on. In 1934, he helped form the Colored Democratic Club. As a representative of that organization, he met with Nevada Senator Patrick McCarran, a meeting that helped obtain jobs for black workers at Boulder Dam. Henry Wilson's obituary didn't do him justice.

Las Vegas Hits the Big Leagues

The annual spring series of major league pre-season baseball games at Cashman Field has sparked interest in the idea of enticing several teams to set up permanent spring training camps in Las Vegas. It may be a marvelous idea, but it certainly isn't a new one. The notion was first floated in 1934 when Las Vegas was still on an economic binge stimulated by Boulder Dam tourism.

Local booster Bob Russell and one "Foghorn" Murphy, a southern California liquor wholesaler, were the chief promoters. Murphy, it appears, was angling for a Pacific Coast League franchise, which would mean, he said, "You can bet your last cent that I'll bring my players here to get in condition." Perhaps he was sampling a little of his own product when he made an alternate suggestion. If spring training didn't work out, he thought maybe that "Irish gang" from Notre Dame would be eager to train here for their annual football battle against USC.

Nineteen thirty-five passed with no spring training and no Fighting Irish. One Pacific Coast League team was reported to be interested. Plans were readied for building locker rooms and showers at the War Memorial Building adjacent to the city park baseball diamond. Planting some grass in the dirt infield was also a possibility. A committee headed by *Review-Journal* sports editor John Cahlan swung into action.

The issue then sank out of sight for a decade. The city thought it got a break in 1944. City Manager Charles McCall was a pal of Pittsburgh Pirates manager Frankie Frisch. A letter to Frisch brought Pirates president William Benswanger to Las Vegas for a week as a guest of the community. Benswanger claimed to be studying the proposal seriously, but still no dice. By 1947, four major league clubs were training in the Southwest, and Las Vegans were still hopeful.

Major league baseball finally came to Las Vegas in 1954. Sports fans got to see Bobby Feller of the Cleveland Indians pitch against Sal Maglie of the New York Giants. In Las Vegas' first ever major league game, Willie Mays's bat was silent as the Indians edged the Giants 2-0 at Cashman Field. There was talk after the game of spring training coming to Las Vegas. There's still talk of major league spring training coming to Las Vegas.

Cashman Field

When the Indians and the Giants first brought major league baseball to Cashman Field in 1954, that wasn't the present Cashman Field. The original baseball stadium of that name was built in the late 1940s and was the inspiration of the Las Vegas Elks. In 1947, the Union Pacific Railroad sold to the Elks a 60-acre parcel, including a large chunk of land formerly part of the Old Las Vegas Ranch on North Fifth Street. The Elks got the property for a fraction of its commercial value, with the understanding that they would develop a multi-purpose stadium.

Work began on the new facility early in 1948 with the hauling of fill dirt from the old racetrack at the city park a short distance away. It was a race against the clock, as the annual Helldorado rodeo was scheduled there for the middle of May. Much of the work was performed by volunteers, by no means all of them Elks. Elk leader Jim Cashman, after whom the field was named, was generous in his praise of more than nine hundred individuals who eventually contributed time and labor. It was estimated that without donated work and materials, the project would have cost citizens a half a million dollars. Actual cash costs were about one fifth of that.

The dedication of the stadium went off as planned before five thousand spectators in May 1948. A Union Pacific official presented the deed to Elks exalted ruler Oscar Bryan, and actor Victor Jory made the dedicatory speech. The rodeo started on schedule the next day.

Still, it took a lot of donations and kangaroo court fees for the Elks to retire the debt. They made considerable progress, but in 1950 they threw in the towel and got the city to take over operation. Evidently the city was none too diligent. In 1956, after the third annual Giants-Indians pre-season contest, club owners threatened never to return because of the condition of the field. Cleveland third baseman Al Rosen was blunt: "You'd better leave me at home next year if we come here again." Teammate Dale Mitchell added: "It's the worst I've ever seen."

It couldn't have been too bad. The teams returned in 1957, and old Cashman Field served adequately until replaced by the present beautiful facility.

The Wranglers and One for the Record Book

If the real beginning of spring is the umpire's first call to "Play Ball," spring finally came to Las Vegas in 1947. A group of local businessmen, including Bob Peccole as president

The 1947 Las Vegas Wranglers set a minor league record for most home runs in a season.

and Louis Wiener as chairman of the board, incorporated Las Vegas' first professional baseball team early that year.

Originally to be called the "Braves" because of its affiliation with Boston's National League team, the team took the field as the "Wranglers." In a city-wide contest, that name won out over such other suggestions as the "Fremont Blues," the "Las Vegas Suns," and the "Sons o' Guns."

After a stint of spring training at Sawtelle, California, playing manager Newt Kimball led his crew of mostly Californian players into their first outing in the Class C

Sunset League, an 8-2 victory over El Centro, California. The home opener five days later was a triumph over the Reno Silver Sox. At that special event, individual players received prizes donated by local businesses. Pitcher Neal Montank won a Stetson hat for the first run scored, and second baseman Paul Godfrey took home a box of cigars for the first infield assist.

Nineteen forty-seven was probably the Wranglers' peak year. Calvin "the Cat" Felix hit fifty-two home runs and Ken "Howitzer" Myers and Olin, no nickname, Kelly added thirty-three each. A thirty-to-five rout of Ontario, California that

May was one for the record books. The Wranglers hit ten home runs, four of them by Ken Myers. Three bases-loaded homers in the third inning is said to be still a record for professional baseball.

The team's financial performance didn't equal their prowess on the field. They lost money each season, though nearly breaking even in 1951. The next spring, there was an eleventh hour plea for support. "Baseball IS a part of community life," an editorial in the *Review-Journal* proclaimed, "an integral and necessary part." The campaign brought in two thousand dollars, enough cash to keep the team afloat one more season in the Class D Southwest International League. After that, Las Vegans had to settle for televised baseball until the San Diego Padres-affiliated Stars came to town.

Horse Racing

Hialeah. Santa Anita. Las Vegas Park. You don't have to be a horse race plunger to recognize the first two. But Las Vegas Park? It almost happened.

Joe Smoot, onetime owner of Hialeah and the man who began construction on Santa Anita, thought Las Vegas was ripe for the sport of kings in 1946. He announced that construction would begin early the following year on a first-rate two-and-a-half million dollar racing facility. It was in fact three years before Smoot selected the noted African-American architect Paul Williams of Los Angeles to begin designing the track. Williams would work with Arthur Froehlich, designer of Hollywood Park.

The location would be in Paradise Valley one quarter mile south of the city limits; that is, near

The drawings in this brochure are architectural projections by Walter Zick, A.I.A. and Harris Sharp, A.I.A. of the plant of the Las Vegas Thoroughbred Racing Association.

where the Convention Center sits today. Actual construction began in May 1950. The first signs of trouble appeared in December as building trades workers threw up picket lines against the McNeil Construction Company. McNeil accepted the challenge by obtaining an injunction against the unions. Labor disputes dragged through the courts into 1951, when evidence of more serious difficulties surfaced.

District Attorney Roger Foley issued a forgery complaint against

Seymour Vorhis, the secretary of the Las Vegas Thoroughbred Racing Association. The young man in turn screamed to the press that he was not going to be a fall guy. Vorhis alleged that he had been asked to sign checks for Association President Joe Smoot and other large stockholders for expensive weekend sprees on the Las Vegas Strip. Stockholders had diverted tens of thousands of dollars into

---

[**1860**] [**1900**] [**1920**]

1875 1ST KENTUCKY DERBY   1891 BASKETBALL INVENTED   1912 1ST BASEBALL STRIKE   1929 RODEO ASSOCIATION FORMED
1898 1ST WOMAN PRO-BASEBALL PLAYER   1920 APFA FORMED (LATER NFL)

1839
Abner Doubleday is credited with inventing Baseball in Cooperstown N.Y. This "fact" is disputed, and Doubleday never claims it himself.

1896
The first modern Olympics is held in Athens, Greece.

1903
First World Series is played (Boston Pilgrims beat the Pittsburgh Pirates).

1910
In Reno, heavyweight champion boxer Jack Johnson bests Jim Jeffries. Dubbed "the great white hope," Jeffries' defeat leads to race riots across

the nation, leaving 11 dead.

1919
Sir Barton is the first horse to win the Triple Crown.

1925
First black baseball team organized in Las Vegas.

1927
First annual New Year's Rodeo held in Las Vegas.

Las Vegas get its first high school football team, the Wildcats.

Babe Ruth hits 60 home runs in a single season; sets new record.

1932
Wildcats high school basketball scandal.

1933
Seabiscuit is born.

1936
Hitler opens the Olympic Games in Berlin.

Jesse Owens, African-American, wins four gold medals and breaks three world records in track and field events.

Left: A Las Vegas Thoroughbred Racing Association brochure, 1950s. Above: Horse racing in Las Vegas.

Smoot and other directors were under indictment for forgery and embezzlement. The charges were later dropped, but the Racing Association was in receivership, the track needed up to a million dollars for completion, and the organization had just $3,000 in cash. The great race track loomed half-finished in the desert looking like the temple of Ozymandias.

What seemed to be the salvation of the project came about because of a chance meeting in San Francisco between Lou Smith and Alfred Luke. Smith was the operator of famed Rockingham Park in New Hampshire, and Luke was prominent in California racing circles. The two came up with a plan to raise two million dollars to finish and open the bankrupt Las Vegas track. Smith, a major investor, became president of the Las Vegas Jockey Club while Luke handled the business end. Webb Everett of Santa Anita, said to be highly regarded among owners, trainers, and jockeys, organized stakes and purses.

their own pockets through other schemes, he claimed.

Nineteen fifty-two opened on a disheartening note. Five years after the first confident announcement,

---

Jesse Owens

Construction began again in the spring of 1953, and the Jockey Club planned a racing season for early September. It was, for little Las Vegas, an extremely ambitious undertaking — comfortable seating for 20,000, a clubhouse, a swank restaurant, an escalator, and stables for a thousand horses. There were to be sixty-seven days of racing with very attractive purses.

The Friday opening drew a crowd of 8,000, but the number dropped to 3,000 by Monday. The fans did see some exciting racing. America's leading jockey, Willie Shoemaker, rode two winners, and the previous year's champ, Anthony DeSpirito, won three. There were a few problems. For one, racing was still going on at Delmar and other California tracks, and many owners passed up the Las Vegas opening. Also, the fancy tote board refused to inform bettors of the odds.

More ominously, the daily handle was less than half of the $400,000 needed to break even. Officials called a temporary suspension of racing until a new board could be installed. Despite reassurances by the Jockey Club, some owners headed back to California. Racing resumed and the new board functioned perfectly, but only for nine more days. Lawsuits emanating from unpaid contractors led to the padlocking of the splendid track in October. Barley was planted on the track to keep it from blowing away. Whether the barley ever sprouted is unknown. What did sprout there eventually was the Las Vegas Convention Center and

a giant hotel, now called the Las Vegas Hilton.

Basketball Scandal

It was the worst sports scandal of the decade in Southern Nevada. Allegations flew that the basketball team's star player was ineligible to enroll and was in school only because of his athletic ability. "You'll be taken care of if you come here to play," the coach was said to have promised. No, it happened a long time ago and it wasn't the Runnin' Rebels.[1] It was more like the movie "Horsefeathers" in which Groucho Marx, as Professor Wagstaff, recruits barflies Chico and Harpo as ringers on the Huxley College football team.

It began in the final frantic days of the season before the state high school basketball championship in 1932. The first hint of a problem came in late February after the Las Vegas Wildcats had defeated the quintet from Lincoln County High School in Panaca by a score of 19-16. The Lincoln County coach explained that, while he didn't want to offer any alibis, his star center had been playing with serious charges hanging over his head. Apparently, someone had told Lincoln County School Board member Henry Lee that the player had been recruited from Utah and was ineligible because he had higher standing than high school.

Lee investigated and turned the results of his study over to the board. The timing was crucial. Lincoln County stood in second place in the league and would go to the state finals in Reno if they

won their final game at Las Vegas. Just before that critical game, the school board declared the player ineligible. Sympathetic Wildcat coach Douglas Dashiell played only his second-stringers and accepted a 38-18 drubbing. The Lincoln County team looked forward to the·bus ride to Reno.

They didn't count on the state athletic federation. That body ruled the Panacans out of the state tournament. A play-off was quickly arranged in which the Muckers from Tonopah High School defeated Virgin Valley and headed north instead. As it turned out, Reno won the game and the championship, but that wasn't the end of the story. Allegations were made that Tonopah's star guard was also a ringer. Especially galling to the Panacans was the fact that Tonopah's principal had voted to declare the Lincoln County player ineligible.

As for the Lincoln County students, they took the extraordinary step of going on strike, futilely demanding the firing of Henry Lee, whom they blamed for the whole mess. The ending will come as no surprise to present day Las Vegans. The Lincoln and Tonopah coaches were fired, the principals were exonerated, and everyone soon forgot about it.

Wildcat Football

During Thanksgiving week in years past, football placed a close second in public enthusiasm to turkey and cranberry sauce. This was especially true in Las Vegas in 1927. This was the year that the Las Vegas High

School Wildcats fielded their first football team.

That September, twenty-three young athletes showed up for practice at a newly cleared field out in the desert near Seventh and Bridger where a new Las Vegas High School would soon be built. Their new coach, Frank Butcher, was optimistic about the team's chances, though none of his players had ever played football. Few had ever even seen a game. Just a week later the team had its first scrimmage. The first-string team won be a score of 12-0 over an aggregation of bench-warmers and local residents. This first organized football contest in Las Vegas wasn't played under game conditions: the team had no equipment and the goal posts hadn't been installed yet.

In early October, a five-game schedule was announced, and on the twenty-fifth, the team lost a squeaker to Victorville, California. A week later, the Wildcats held a much heavier and more experienced Kingman, Arizona team to a two-touchdown victory. Kingman responded by drubbing Las Vegas 70-7 the following week in Arizona. On Thanksgiving Day 1927, the Wildcats won their first game, beating Panaca 13-12. An easy victory later over the same team rounded out a surprisingly successful first season.

Just three years later the Wildcats went five-and-one and might have won the state championship, but Reno passed up the chance to travel to Las Vegas for a game. But that football season ended tragically. Coach Frank Butcher was severely burned in a fire at his home in early December and died a few days later. The football field at the new high school long carried his name.

Chapter Notes

[1] This piece on basketball was originally written during a late phase of the extended legal conflict involving the National Collegiate Athletic Association, the University of Nevada, Las Vegas, and the university's basketball coach, Jerry Tarkanian.

Chapter EIGHT

Working Men and Women

The Railroad Strike of 1922

Until Las Vegas began to explore its tourism potential in the 1930s, the local economy was geared to the railroad payroll. Accordingly, a rail strike in 1922 dealt a severe blow, as local shop workers and electricians joined a national walkout. At first, the effects were quite mild: trains ran late, and the city went for a time without electricity, since the railroad supplied the city's power.

In mid-summer, the situation worsened. Seven men brought in to replace striking workers were taken from a train, beaten, and sent back to Los Angeles. The trainmaster, who iced the trains personally, was given a coat of tar. The violence brought a concerned Governor Boyle to town. He arrived in time to assist personally in the arrest of seventeen men for shooting firearms near the compound where non-striking employees stayed. Local merchants agreed with union leaders that a small minority was responsible for the violence. Taking no chances, the governor called in a small contingent of state officers to keep the peace.

Throughout the strike, which lasted until October, residents were sympathetic to the strikers. Benefit concerts and an amateur theatrical performance drew large crowds to Fremont Street. Settlement of the strike didn't bring the expected benefits. The Union Pacific had decided to close the railroad shops so crucial to local prosperity. Las Vegas settled into a slump from which it only slowly emerged. The construction of Boulder Dam and the thousands of sightseers that it brought gave the town a new orientation in the next decade.

The Central Labor Council

Labor Day 1929 was a day of great celebration for the working men and women of Las Vegas. The city had just experienced the most intensive period of labor organization in its history.

It had begun with the signing in December 1928 by President Calvin Coolidge of the bill authorizing the construction of Boulder Dam. Job seekers flooded into town. Just three months later, a new labor union organized, as

Las Vegas railroad workers in the 1920s.

the Painters, Decorators and Paperhangers received their charter from the American Federation of Labor. Immediately following this great pre-construction rush, came the organization of the carpenters, barbers, plumbers, laborers, hod carriers, culinary workers, and plasterers. Suddenly, hundreds of workers were newly organized in the small desert town.

This organizing effort was crowned in August 1929 with the creation of the Las Vegas Central Labor Council. With just under a month to go before Labor Day, the Council set about planning a grand celebration. Labor Day exceeded expectations. The day began with a parade down Fremont Street, with the American Legion drum corps leading marching groups representing the various unions. Then, there was racing, swimming, and a beauty contest at Lorenzi's Resort, Judge Roger Foley spoke, as did District Attorney Harley Harmon, who expressed pride in his twenty-seven years of union membership. Dancing at Lorenzi's ballroom capped the event.

The new Central Labor Council won its first battle, obtaining the appointment of a deputy labor commissioner for Southern Nevada. Commissioner Leonard Blood established that office in November 1930. There were successes and failures in the difficult years that followed, but the excitement of 1929 was seldom matched.

Culinary Union

The Culinary Union, like many other Las Vegas craft unions, traces its roots back to Depression-era Las Vegas. Local cooks and waiters first banded together to form Local 591 in early October 1931. Less than three weeks later, its first president, Bert Simpson, was in jail for disorderly conduct.

The union had first targeted restaurants and cafes, where wages were $7 a day for waiters. Waitresses settled for a dollar less. Simpson had been arrested for allegedly using "vile language" in discouraging diners from patronizing the White Spot Cafe. He resigned as union president two days later. That was the day that restaurant owners demanded, and received from the city commission, an emergency anti-picketing ordinance. Declaring that picketing was a "racket," the commission prohibited any conduct which might influence patrons to refrain from buying goods from

an establishment. Nonetheless, the wage dispute was amicably settled within a few days, as all restaurant owners signed contracts with the union.

The fight against the anti-picketing ordinance was less successful. In April 1932, union member Harry

Mardis was jailed for picketing. His lawyer argued that the city ordinance conflicted with state statutes, which permitted peaceful picketing. In an argument that defied ordinary logic, district judge William Orr upheld the conviction, saying that while picketing is lawful, the city

White Spot Cafe workers lined up for their pay in silver dollars in the 1940s.

be widespread dissatisfaction with wages. Musicians first organized in September of the following year. Pianist Jack Tenny, noted as the composer of "Mexicali Rose," became the first union president. During the first couple of years, the union mostly concerned itself with meetings and benefit dances at the Venetian Ballroom, a popular nickel-a-dance place on First Street. It was reported that most of the members were working regularly.

In 1934, as the Depression deepened and the Boulder Dam construction boom began to peter out, the situation was much worse. Many orchestra members were making just one dollar a day. Musicians urged the city commission to repeal an ordinance requiring taverns to close at midnight; longer hours would permit them to make a living wage. The commissioners took a firmly middle of the road position, calling upon tavern owners to increase wages while refusing to extend tavern hours. The next day, the musicians met on the courthouse lawn and reorganized as Local 369.

From that point, the union became more active. A brief dispute with Lorenzi's Lake Resort over the signing of a contract was resolved after much argument in the press. In July 1935, simmering grievances at Boulder Dam led to a walkout there, and union orchestras organized benefits for the striking workers. It was a difficult period for everyone, but at least the musicians didn't have to worry then, as they do now, about being replaced by a tape recorder or synthesizer.

can enact any legislation necessary to protect peace and good order. The decision apparently took the steam out of local 591 and it faded away. Local 226, the present organization, was created three years later in 1935.

The Musicians Union

Newspapers probably exaggerated a bit when they reported in 1930 that Las Vegas musicians made seven dollars for a three-hour set. Still, in that early year of the Great Depression, there didn't seem to

Black Labor at Boulder Dam

In the light of 1990s decisions by the U.S. Supreme Court limiting affirmative action plans in employment, it is enlightening to look back at the Boulder Dam construction era. In 1930, the population of Las Vegas was about 5,000; of these, 143 Las Vegans were black. None of them were hired in the early phases of the huge project. At a time when labor unions were beginning to win small advances for their members, black workers ran into a stone wall.

The black community responded in May 1931 by forming the Colored Citizens' Labor Protective Association. Its purpose was to provide competent employees in all vocations. In spite of meetings with local officials and appeals in the newspapers, there were still no black workers at the Dam. In a Las Vegas speech in 1932, a national representative of the National Association of Colored People castigated the Hoover administration for its failure to provide for the hiring of blacks. Archie Cross, federal employment director for Nevada, gave a curious response: the construction company didn't want to have to build a separate dormitory for them. Besides, there were only two hundred black job seekers locally and there were many more unemployed white workers!

Finally, in late June 1932, Six Companies president W.A. Bechtel got the message. With a little nudge from Nevada Senator Tasker Oddie, Bechtel promised to hire black workers. Between July and September, twenty-four blacks were hired to work in the Arizona gravel pits. Considering the thousands who worked at the Dam, it was a small achievement.

One Big Union

"One Big Union" was the rallying cry of the Industrial Workers of the World. The Wobblies, as they were called, proclaimed a radical program of labor strikes leading eventually to worker control of the means of production. The IWW was founded in 1905 and staged its first major organizational efforts that same year in the Nevada mining camps of Tonopah and Goldfield. Despite their radical goal, the Wobblies, at least in Nevada, spent most of their efforts on bread-and-butter issues — wages, hours, and working conditions. Even so, the IWW was suppressed by federal troops in Goldfield in 1907.

In 1931, the IWW was active at the new Boulder Dam construction site. On July 10, Wobbly organizer Frank Anderson was arrested for vagrancy as he sold IWW newspapers in downtown Las Vegas. From jail, Anderson claimed that three hundred men had already been signed up at the dam. Alarmed local newspaper editors overlooked the fact that the issues were far from radical. The union man protested hazardous working conditions, the lack of fresh drinking water, and intolerable heat in the workingmen's barracks.

Over the next few days, more organizers were arrested, but a courageous Las Vegas judge ordered the vagrancy charges dismissed. Further organizational efforts met with little success however; most dam workers chose to avoid affiliation with the Wobblies. Whatever

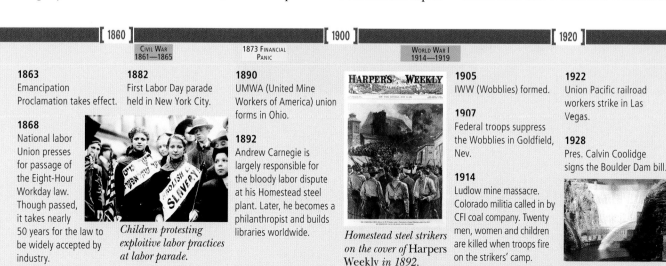

[1860] CIVIL WAR 1861—1865   1873 FINANCIAL PANIC   [1900]   WORLD WAR I 1914—1919   [1920]

1863
Emancipation Proclamation takes effect.

1868
National labor Union presses for passage of the Eight-Hour Workday law. Though passed, it takes nearly 50 years for the law to be widely accepted by industry.

Children protesting exploitive labor practices at labor parade.

1882
First Labor Day parade held in New York City.

1890
UMWA (United Mine Workers of America) union forms in Ohio.

1892
Andrew Carnegie is largely responsible for the bloody labor dispute at his Homestead steel plant. Later, he becomes a philanthropist and builds libraries worldwide.

Homestead steel strikers on the cover of Harpers Weekly *in 1892.*

1905
IWW (Wobblies) formed.

1907
Federal troops suppress the Wobblies in Goldfield, Nev.

1914
Ludlow mine massacre. Colorado militia called in by CFI coal company. Twenty men, women and children are killed when troops fire on the strikers' camp.

1922
Union Pacific railroad workers strike in Las Vegas.

1928
Pres. Calvin Coolidge signs the Boulder Dam bill.

influence the IWW wielded at Boulder Dam ended in August during a brief strike over reduced wages. The Wobblies played only a minor role and the strike was broken easily. Except for a few isolated actions, this was the last gasp of the "one big union."

The Working Man is Poor

> *The gambling man is rich and the working man is poor.*

Depression-era balladeer Woody Guthrie wasn't thinking of Las Vegas when he wrote those words, but he might as well have been. Most accounts of Las Vegas in the 1930s stress the prosperity created by Boulder Dam construction and the thrill of open gambling. Those aspects were real.

But a different side of Las Vegas at the time can be seen in a 1930 photograph of a young man, two small children on his arm, as he milked a burro. The photographer, Winthrop Davis, recorded the man's words: "My wife has left this troubled world due to the lack of proper medical care, and

Americans seeking jobs on the Boulder Dam project produced many "rag town" scenes like this one in the 1930s.

what you're looking at is all I have except a bag of corn meal. Pray for me, brother."

For those lucky enough or determined enough to get and keep a construction job on the Dam, life in Las Vegas was good. But for the jobless men who slept in Union Pacific Park, the bright lights of the casinos just across the street on Fremont were part of a different world.

Nearly a thousand slept in "Hoover City," a ragtown encampment at the edge of the cemetery. For the forty or fifty men who arrived with each freight train, there were the "hobo jungles" by Las Vegas Creek.

The employment line was hopelessly long. The Salvation Army bread line was longer. Local leaders said it was the longest in the United States. In October 1930, while the official

---

[1930]	[1940]	[1950]
The Great Depression 1933 Roosevelt Creates CCC, 1935 WPA	US in World War II 1941—1945	

Presidential candidate Herbert Hoover declares the end of poverty, "closer than ever." He wins the presidency in a landslide. The Great Depression begins on Hoover's watch.

1929
Las Vegas Central Labor Council formed.

1931
Culinary Workers Union formed.

1932
First unemployment insurance law (Wisconsin).

1934
Henry Wilson helps to organize the Colored Democratic Club in an effort to win jobs for black men at Boulder Dam.

1935
Wagner Act guarantees workers collective bargaining.

1935-40
Union membership doubles to 7.3 million. Declining membership will begin in the '60s with changing conditions.

1936
Supreme Court reverses earlier decision and rules Minimum Wage Law constitutional.

1938
CIO breaks from AFL.

1940
Twenty-seven percent of women work outside of home.

1943
BMI in Henderson employs women as an experiment.

1944
Thirty-five percent of women in the labor force during the war years.

1945
Returning veterans displace women workers.

1955
AFL and CIO merge again and spur some renewed growth in union membership.

1965
Martin Luther King Jr. leads the March on Washington, a historic civil rights demonstration.

population of Las Vegas was just over five thousand and even before there were jobs on the Dam, nearly eleven thousand people asked for help. Las Vegas police struggled to make the problem go away by making the people go away. First, it was the threat of thirty days in jail; then they trucked indigents to Los Angeles. Finally, it was a Westside stockade and the chain gang.

The final words of Guthrie's ballad would have echoed in every heart:

The po-lice they are hard, wherever I may go.

And I ain't got no home in this world any more.

CIO

The Congress of Industrial Organizations was organized in 1935 within the American Federation of Labor. Conflicts with the parent organization were apparent by 1937. The CIO was organized in Southern Nevada that June, and by November, AFL workers were picketing Las Vegas food stores that had signed CIO contracts. The break between the two labor groups was complete in 1938. Leo Flynn, a national AFL figure, told the state convention that year that the rival CIO was controlled by communists. The *Review-Journal,* a Democratic newspaper more sympathetic to the AFL, splashed the story across its front page.

The conflict also had a political dimension. Nevada's powerful Senator Patrick McCarran, who had distanced himself from the foreign policy of President Franklin Roos-

evelt, received ardent AFL support. The CIO strongly supported FDR and was bitterly anti-McCarran.

In May 1943, the CIO-affiliated Mine, Mill and Smelter Workers forced a labor election among workers at the giant magnesium plant at Henderson. To everyone's surprise, the workers favored the CIO over the AFL by a significant margin. With McCarran at least tacitly supporting the Federation, the War Labor Board finally declined jurisdiction, and the CIO was denied its victory.

The CIO almost gained retribution the following year. In one of the nastiest campaigns in Nevada history, McCarran charged his Democratic opponent, Lieutenant Governor Vail Pittman, with being a tool for establishing CIO control of Nevada. With CIO support, the Clark County Democratic Convention refused to endorse the Senator. Only with intense effort and a great deal of mudslinging did he manage to retain his seat and his tight grip on Nevada politics.

Rosie the Riveter Comes to Nevada

Southern Nevada's first large industrial facility, Basic Magnesium, Incorporated at Henderson, stimulated major demographic changes in the Las Vegas area. Thousands of new workers, a large percentage of them black, overwhelmed available housing. A less remarked effect of BMI was the first use in Southern Nevada of women workers on the production line.

During World War II, "Rosie the Riveter" symbolized the many

thousands of American women filling plant and factory vacancies created by the voracious appetite of the Selective Service System. Rosie's career in Southern Nevada began in February 1943.

Plant construction had begun in the fall of 1941. The first shipments of magnesium for incendiary bombs, tracer bullets and alloyed steel were made less than a year later. Partly because of difficult living and working conditions, the absentee and attrition rate among workers was extremely high. The plant newspaper, *The Big Job,* complained that during one week in January 1943, there were more than 2,500 absent workers. It was about then that plant managers decided upon an "experiment" to see what kinds of production jobs women could perform.

Edna Mae Pierce was the first. In early February, she went to work as an ingot handler. Within days, fifteen other women were working on production jobs on all three shifts. As in other communities, the new plant workers were mostly housewives who were wage earners for the first time. Soon, it was common for the newsletter to show photos of women working in potentially hazardous jobs in the metals and chlorination units. Rosie the Riveter had begun to change the way Southern Nevada families lived.

Organizing the Dealers

In early 2001, dealers at Las Vegas casinos and resorts made a run at organizing casino floors under the auspices of the Transport Workers. In union certification elections, the union won a couple, lost more. This wasn't the first unionization attempt on the part of dealers, however.

In June 1964, Tom Hanley's new union, the American Federation of Casino Gaming Employees, challenged the Nevada Resort Association by holding a series of rallies aimed at organizing dealers, change girls, and slot mechanics. Ominously, this was more than a two-way struggle. Hanley, a scarred veteran of bitter fights within the Sheet Metal Workers Union, simultaneously took on the 9,000-member Culinary Union and its local boss, Al Bramlet. In Hanley's view, Bramlet's simultaneous flirtation with the dealers was part of a

conspiracy with the resort industry to block his Federation.

The issues were complex; Hanley pointed to twelve years of wage stagnation, arbitrary firings, abusive labor practices, and violations of federal maximum hour regulations. Resorts fired back with charges of labor racketeering and claims of poverty in the highly competitive gaming market. Hanley boasted that his federation had already enlisted more than half the dealers in ten Strip and Downtown casinos.

The first representation elections didn't come until mid-1965. Dealers at the El Dorado in Henderson and at the Showboat on Boulder Highway rejected both unions be-

fore the Federation won the right to represent workers at North Las Vegas' Bonanza Club. In the end, that victory was the only one, and that union pact lasted just one year until the Bonanza folded.

There is a deadly postscript. In the midst of a more personal struggle in 1977, Al Bramlet was taken into the desert and shot to death. Convicted of his murder, Tom Hanley died in custody while waiting to testify in a union corruption trial.

A dealer works a roulette wheel at the Las Vegas Club in 1940.

Potpourri

Electrifying Las Vegas

During the heat waves of mid-summer in Southern Nevada, Nevada Power Company regularly announces new daily records in the use of electrical power. Las Vegans have probably become a bit blasé about their massive consumption of electricity and probably flinch only a little when bill-paying time comes. By contrast, the knotty problem of getting even barely adequate power was almost an obsession with Las Vegans in the first years of the town.

Las Vegas was born in May 1905, but it wasn't until December that wiring of the town for electricity was even begun. Finally, in February 1906, the power plant at the railroad icehouse began operation and residents could turn on electric lights for the first time. Not that this was an occasion for much celebration; the power was available for only a short time in the evening.

Fully a year later, the Consolidated Power and Telephone Company spent $20,000 on a new power generating system and in August 1907, the lights got a little brighter. So encouraged by this development was the power company that the wiring of Fremont Street for street lighting was begun on an "experimental" basis in 1908. There was, of course, no power for air conditioning during the daylight hours, but then there wasn't any air conditioning either. The more affluent residents, at least those whose jobs prevented their leaving for the summer, could order a Kenco fan from the Sears catalogue and a twenty-cell battery with which to power it. The fifty-two-pound package cost a whopping $8.75.

In the summer of 1914, the power company demonstrated some mercy as they provided daytime power on a temporary basis. Two years later, the company retired its ancient generating plant and began purchasing power from the railroad's powerful facility. Thus, the company was finally able to provide twenty-four-hour electric power nearly eleven years after the town's founding. The old generator was called out of retirement briefly during an extended railroad strike in 1922,[1] when the Las Vegans again did without power for their fans during the sweltering summer days. Incidentally, those streetlights, wired so hopefully in 1908, were finally turned on in 1913. They provided the first tentative flickers to what would become "Glitter Gulch."

Convention City

From its founding in 1936, the Las Vegas Junior Chamber of Commerce has been one of the city's most active civic organizations. Its early philanthropic efforts included sponsoring classical music concerts and staging dances to benefit undernourished children. In light of the huge conventions that now convene regularly in Las Vegas, it's interesting to recall the Jaycees' role in hosting the city's first large convention. In 1937, a delegation of Las Vegas Jaycees traveled to the regional conference in San Diego.

A leading Jaycee and one of the delegates was Paul Ralli. Ralli was one of Las Vegas' more interesting and civic-minded denizens. He had left an acting career during which he had appeared on the stage opposite Mae West and on the screen with Marion Davies. He came to Nevada to pass the bar exam and became a Las Vegas divorce attorney. It was largely his quick thinking that enabled the Las Vegas contingent to lure six hundred of their fellows to Las Vegas for the 1938 convention.

As Ralli later told the story, he had spent a long night plying a group of delegates with whiskey. The next morning, he found himself still inebriated and clinging precariously to a lamppost as a woman delegate passed. Clearly appalled, the matron demanded to know what city he represented. "T-T-Tucson," he was able to stammer. In the polling for host city honors shortly thereafter, Las Vegas bested Tucson by one vote, including that of the deluded woman.

The convention itself included the usual Old West-style high jinks. The most anticipated event was the dog-versus-badger fight to be held on Fremont Street. The Las Vegas Jaycees proclaimed themselves determined to prove that their most vicious dog was more than a match for a champion badger from Ely.

After a massive publicity build-up in the local press and contrary to the express wishes of city and county law enforcement, the match went off as scheduled before two thousand spectators. An unsuspecting delegate was selected to dress himself in heavy clothes, and pull on stovepipes to his knees (by way of armor.) Then he was to grab a rope, yank Ely's angry badger from its cage, and run like hell. All went as planned; it took some time to soothe the poor sap's nerves — even after he discovered that he had only a clattering metal chamber pot at the other end of the rope. He was far from the first victim of this old mining camp prank.

This first large convention in Las Vegas was declared a great success, an auspicious beginning for Las Vegas as a convention destination. Another major turning point came in April 1959. Variety Club International was hosting its annual convention in Las Vegas. Fifteen hundred delegates from around the world gathered for the first convention to be held at Las Vegas' new five-million-dollar convention center. By all reports, the extravagant performance staged for the participants in the rotunda of the new building was a resounding success. That was just a warm-up though for the main event: the enormous World Congress of Flight.

This was a good deal more than a little merriment on Fremont Street. For a week beginning April 12, 1959, Las Vegas was the stage for the exhibition of the latest in military and commercial aviation. From intercontinental ballistic mis-siles like the Atlas to tiny aircraft built entirely of rubber, from giant airplanes like the B-52 bomber to the swiftest of new jet fighters, all were on display to the public. A massive display of firepower at Indian Springs Air Base climaxed the week. All of this was conveyed to the entire nation via special reports on NBC Television. It was a splendid kick-off for Las Vegas' convention center and just a small preview of later conventions that would sometimes bring more than a hundred thousand visitors to town.

Is it "Helldorado" or "Heldorado"?

Unless you count the myriad lights of the Fremont Street canopy, Glitter Gulch has probably seen its last real live parade. The first Helldorado parade of sixty-one years ago was not the street's first parade, but it was the inauguration of a tradition that continued in some form until fairly recently. In the spring of 1935, the news everywhere was grim — killer dust storms in the Midwest, jobless and starving Chicagoans, striking autoworkers in Detroit — but little of this had an echo in Las Vegas. Boulder Dam was just completed and the one-time whistle-stop of Las Vegas had seen nearly 125,000 visitors in the first four months alone. It was time for a celebration.

Led by the Elks Lodge, Las Vegas threw the biggest party in its thirty-year history and called it Helldorado. For four days, civic leaders donned gaudy Western clothing, held kangaroo courts, and elbowed up to the eighty-foot bar

The Helldorado celebration drew many floats to Fremont Street.

in a specially constructed Frontier Village. Women in pioneer garb competed for the title of Belle of Helldorado. Fifteen hundred costumes were rented from Paramount Studios. There was one caveat: local participants were cautioned not to carry firearms. Stars of the occasion were Searchlight rancher and Hollywood actor Rex Bell, and the celebrated desert rat, Death Valley Scotty.

Advertised all over the Southwest, Helldorado was an enormous success and became an annual affair. The next year a rodeo was added and Tex Ritter starred in the first of a long series of Helldorado appearances. In 1946, the event drew national attention with the filming here of the movie "Heldorado," with Roy Rogers, Dale Evans and Gabby Hayes. The name was a little too risque for Hollywood of the 1940s, so they softened its impact by dropping one of the l's from Helldorado. At a time when Las Vegas was just beginning to flex its tourism muscle, the Helldorado celebration helped create a public-

---

Timeline

[1900]   [1920]   [1940]

CIVIL WAR 1861—1865 | 1906 SAN FRANCISCO EARTHQUAKE | WORLD WAR I 1914—1919 | 1924 1ST WINTER OLYMPICS | WORLD WAR II 1941 MT. RUSHMORE FINISHED

1866
The first official Nevada State Seal adopted.

1902
Willis Carrier invents the modern air conditioning system.

1907
Nevada's first Chamber of Commerce established in Elko.

1918-1919
Influenza pandemic kills 550,000 Americans. Twenty-five million die worldwide.

1921
First Miss America contest held in Atlantic City, N.J.

1922
Minnesotan Ralph Samuelson invents the sport of water skiing. It later becomes popular on Lake Mead.

1935
First Helldorado celebration held.

Las Vegas hosts its first convention.

1939
World's Fair in New York themed "The World of Tomorrow."

1944
Severe drought leads to empty wells in Las Vegas Valley.

1945
Everything atomic is popular. Kix cereal offers a toy "Atomic Bomb Ring" for 15¢ and a box top.

1946
Vegas Vic appears in magazine ads.

1948
Vegas Vic becomes the mascot for the LV Chamber of Commerce.

1949
USSR tests first atomic bomb.

1951
Duck-and-cover drills mandatory in schools. Fallout shelters become popular backyard items.

Vegas Vic sign goes up at the Pioneer Club.

ity image of Las Vegas as the last frontier of the real Wild West.

Water

Las Vegans have always been profligate in their use of water. From its founding in 1905, boosters touted the valley as an agricultural paradise situated atop an inexhaustible lake of underground water. Almost every week, the newspaper featured a story on a gushing new well. By 1911, over seventy wells flowed — unchecked. That was the year that the state engineer first urged Las Vegans to curb their lavish waste of water.

The warning went largely unheeded. By the mid-1930s there were about three hundred wells. In March 1935, the issue of capping the wells was introduced in the state legislature by Clark County Assemblyman Pat Cline. The legislators yawned and went home. Las Vegas residents were then using about 650 gallons of water per person per day. In 1939, the legislature did take the small but important step of requiring a permit to dig a well.

Two years later, residents were using eight hundred gallons a day.

During the years of World War II, resources were strained as never before as the valley's population more than tripled. In the summer of 1944, the shortage was acute. Fire hydrants drew air, and new warnings by state engineer Alfred Merritt Smith were finally taken to heart. A few years later, the legislature authorized the formation of the Las Vegas Valley Water District. One of the new entity's first goals was the acquisition of Lake Mead water from the forty-inch pipeline that had supplied the huge defense plant at Henderson. With that issue resolved by 1952 and the later passage of an $8.7 million bond issue, the District began construction on the linking pipelines. The tap was officially opened into Las Vegas homes in September 1955 providing a respite from perennial water crises for several decades. Periodic dry spells serve as a sharp reminder of how precarious our hold is on our fragile desert environment.

Vegas Vic

Las Vegans and tourists alike are familiar with the towering neon cowboy at the old, now-defunct Pioneer Club on Fremont Street. Residents of some duration can recall when his baritone voice intoned "Howdy Podner" every few minutes. Perhaps fewer residents are aware that the jaunty cowboy has a history predating the construction of the sign in 1951.

From its first organized promotional efforts in the mid-1930s, the Las Vegas Chamber of Commerce utilized Old West themes. A publicity campaign in 1935 created national attention with photos of a prospector's burro registering for a room at the Apache Hotel, precursor of the present Binion's Horseshoe. Ten years later, with the war in Europe winding down, the Chamber mounted a sustained publicity and advertising effort. The well-known firm of J. Walter Thompson at first devised the themes and strategies.

In January 1946, the campaign began to pay off; Las Vegas ads appeared in the *Saturday Evening*

1950-53 Korean War
1955 1st Microwave Ovens
1961 Berlin Wall Built
1989 Berlin Wall Torn Down
1993 WWW Privatized
1999 Y2K Scare

1952 Planned Parenthood, founded by Margaret Sanger in 1916, goes international.

Lake Mead water brought to Las Vegas in pipelines.

1953 Elizabeth II, age 27, crowned queen of Great Britain.

DNA double helix is discovered.

1954 TV dinners first marketed.

1955 Disneyland opens in Anaheim, California.

First consumer model microwave ovens available sold for $1,300.

1958 Wham-O introduces the Hula Hoop.

1959 Mattel Toys introduces the Barbie Doll.

Alaska and Hawaii become the 49th and 50th states.

1966 Howard Hughes moves to Las Vegas' Desert Inn penthouse, where he would stay until 1970. He died on an airplane enroute from Mexico to Houston in 1976.

1960 El Rancho, the first casino on the Strip, burns down. The site of this hotel/casino is still vacant today, at Las Vegas Blvd. and Sahara.

Chubby Checker popularizes dance craze with hit song, *The Twist.* Hula Hoopers dig it.

1964 The Beatles make their American debut on the *Ed Sullivan Show.*

1975 Harvard dropout Bill Gates founds Microsoft.

1984 Macintosh computer introduced by maverick Apple Computer.

Post, Esquire, and other national magazines. The ads touted "fun in the sun" and featured a smiling cowboy jerking his thumb toward Las Vegas. The following year, a new ad firm gave the cowboy a name and a voice — it was Vegas Vic greeting the magazine reader with a cheery "Howdy, podner."

Vegas Vic became the Chamber's trademark, and businesses that contributed to the ad campaign sported Vegas Vic stickers. Neon signs appeared as well, of which the Pioneer Club sign is the most spectacular. One version can still be seen downtown. The Neon Museum rescued the image from the defunct Nevada Motel on Fremont Street and has had it restored. It blazes in full Western glory on Third Street.

"Southwest of Town"

The history of particular Las Vegas neighborhoods can give an appreciation of how the city has developed. A look at the past of one area very close to the downtown core might give an idea of just how small Las Vegas was until after World War II. The area bordering on Charleston Boulevard just west of the railroad tracks was rural into the 1940s. For this remote neighborhood, the telephone book listed no street numbers; addresses there were just "southwest of town."

The predominant smell of the area was manure. To the north of Charleston were the stockyards, while nestled by the tracks across the road, Harry Blanding's slaughterhouse was the source of fresh meat for the city's markets. A little farther west, just past the present freeway, was dairy country. Harry Anderson's Holsteins grazed on the south side of the road, while across the way, George Ullom started up a new dairy for his wife who, for health reasons was advised to drink only Guernsey milk.

Still farther outside the pale of civilization, way out where University Medical Center is today, was the County Poor Farm. The poor farm was, in fact, the ancestor of the present medical complex. In 1924, a shack was hauled from Main Street out "southwest of town," and, with its vegetable garden, it became the poor farm. In 1929, a new building was capable of housing eight or ten elderly or handicapped men. By 1945, the facility had grown into Clark County General Hospital.

In 1913, the eighty acres on the south side of the street very nearly

became Las Vegas' first suburban development. The owner, town mayor Peter Buol, had interested Scottish investors in his Southern Nevada Land and Development Company. Just as the deal was about to be closed, the principal investor died in Scotland. The present exclusive neighborhood, of course, is still referred to as the "Scotch Eighty" after that episode. Take a spin along Rancho Drive through that area and try to imagine it as the bucolic agricultural area it once was. It also might interest you to know that you will be driving over the old railroad grade toward Rhyolite and Goldfield.

Heat

No matter how hot it gets in Las Vegas, it seems that old-timers can always remember when it was a lot hotter. News reports might refer back to July 1942 when the mercury registered 117 degrees. Even on that date, one local resident recalled that it was an unofficial 120 degrees on the day her daughter was born in 1909.

When it gets really hot, one might reflect on the killer heat wave of 1931. Depression era unemployment that year led President Herbert Hoover to speed up the construction of Hoover Dam. Worker housing at Boulder City was not yet ready and hundreds of workers and their families crowded into the ragtown community of Williamsville beside the Colorado River. Temperatures there ran above 120. With poor

Vegas Vic towers above the Pioneer Club on Fremont Street in the 1950s. Far left, A Vegas Vic postcard from 1950s.

drinking water and no electricity for fans, several Williamsville residents died of heat prostration. One Boulder City pioneer recalled bathing her children in the river and building a lean-to of wet sheets for them to play in.

It was even worse for the workers. Temperatures in the airless diversion tunnels under construction reach 140 degrees. In July alone, fourteen workers died from the heat. At first, company officials attributed the deaths to workers' not being accustomed to desert living or to their overeating. The following year, a study by a team of Harvard University scientists revealed that adequate drinking water and the addition of salt to the workers' diet could substantially reduce the incidence of heat prostration. In the meantime, the heat wave of '31 had passed and workers had begun to occupy Boulder City. The crisis was over.

The Cal-Nevada Wars

Las Vegas had gotten bad publicity before, but this was ridiculous. It wasn't the usual innuendo about prostitutes and mobsters, but about the threat of nuclear attack. It was the summer of 1961, a time when school children were drilled to "duck and cover" and home owners scrambled to build fallout shelters in their backyards. A Las Vegas Civil Defense official announced a plan to create a citizen militia of 5,000 men. Its mission would be to protect Nevadans against Californians fleeing atomic attack. "They could come in like a swarm of human locusts," he said, "and pick the valley clean of food, medical supplies and other goods."

Press reaction in California was swift. Headlines screamed "Spenders, Si, Refugees, No!" and "Nevada Set to Repel a Million Californians." Letter writers chimed in: "Las Vegas will have to do without me and my money," was a typical reaction. One California politician proposed building an army of 100,000 to scale the Sierra Nevada and descend upon the cities of Nevada. Sam Boyd of the Las Vegas Chamber of Commerce quickly made placating remarks, and the *Review-Journal* editorialized soothingly about Nevadans' generosity in helping potential nuclear refugees. This seemed to avert a Nevada-California war.

Then, just weeks later, the Nevada Highway Patrol fired a second salvo. Over the busy Labor Day weekend, NHP threw up a roadblock at Jean, a wide spot on Highway 91 from Los Angeles. A thousand Las Vegas-bound Californians were stopped, and traffic snarled as registration and license offenders were cited. Ray Inman, Goodsprings Justice of the Peace, sat in his car in the sweltering heat and dispensed roadside justice. The fines, payable on the spot, were several times higher than normal. Amid the renewed California outcry, the *Review-Journal* editor just threw up his hands. "Let's grow up," he said. We must have: the Californians are still coming.

Chapter Notes

[1] See Chapter 8.

Chapter TEN

Some Military Matters

Gunnery School

Early in 1941, Las Vegas was under serious consideration as the site of an Army Air Forces Gunnery School. There was plenty of federally-owned land and the climate was ideal. It was the climate at city hall that almost stopped the project. There were at the time two bitterly hostile city commissions, each denying the other's legitimacy. Important matters had to be resolved, and the commissions, meeting at opposite ends of city hall, could agree on virtually nothing.

Miraculously, at the end of January 1941 they agreed upon the terms of a lease to the federal government of airport facilities just purchased from Western Air Express. The document was drawn up in duplicate, a copy was signed by each of the two commissions, and sent to Washington.

On February 1, the War Department inked the agree-

The horned toad was the logo for the Las Vegas Army Gunnery School.

ment and the base would be a reality. Well, maybe. Well diggers kept sinking dry holes. Two local businessmen saved the situation by acquiring for the Army water rights to a nearby ranch. The air base was ready for partial occupation by September, but living conditions were terrible because of heat, wind and sand. Resident officers were astonished to find that the

first carload of supplies contained mostly lawnmowers.

Nonetheless, the first gunnery class began its five weeks of training in December and forty-seven gunnery cadets graduated in January. They had trained mostly with old two-seater AT-6 aircraft and BB guns, .22s, and shotguns contributed by the Las Vegas citizenry. Shortages of weapons and planes were eventually overcome, and by war's end, nearly 55,000 aerial gunners had passed through training at the Las Vegas Gunnery School. The school would later become Nellis Air Force Base.

Blackout

At 7:45 p.m. on December 10, 1941, the steam whistle at the Las Vegas railroad yards issued three short blasts followed by a longer one — Morse code signifying "V" for victory. The whistle initiated the second citywide blackout following the Japanese attack on Pearl Harbor

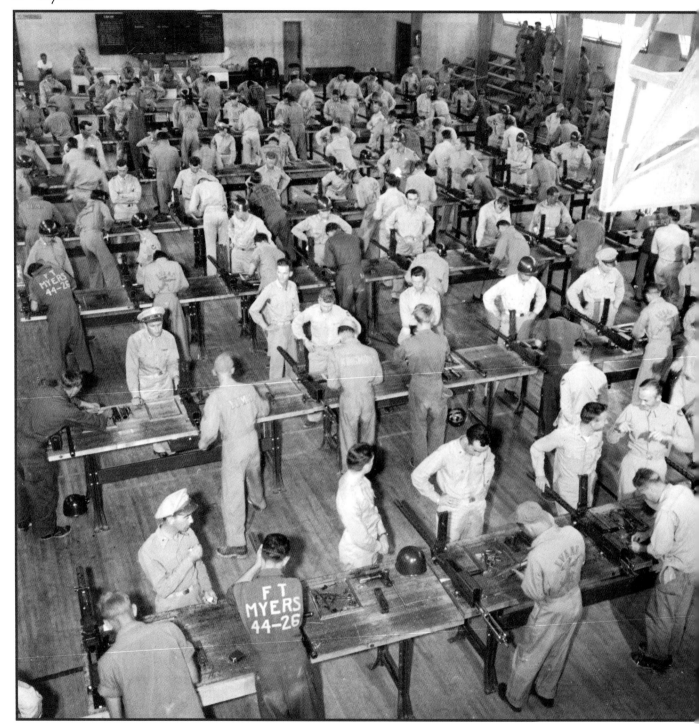

Soldiers from many bases are gathered for training at the Las Vegas Army Gunnery School, assembling machine guns under the gaze of their instructors.

three days earlier. The first test had demonstrated obvious problems: powerhouse lights at Boulder Dam had not been extinguished, nor had the lights at the magnesium plant construction site on Boulder Highway. In town, a band of irate citizens with bricks stormed a residence to smash an offending porch light.

Observation of the blackout on the tenth was much better, though a crowd at J.C. Penney's on Fremont Street complained that the store's lights blazed for eight minutes after

minor inconvenience: members of the Elks Lodge had to suspend their game of pan, and a local minister postponed a wedding at his house.

But the blackout also brought tragedy; two airmen from the new Las Vegas Gunnery School, Lt. John Kelso and Lt. George Turner, died in an unexplained plane crash. The two officers had been flying above the valley during the blackout to check on its effectiveness. The memory of those two servicemen was long preserved in the Kelso-Turner neighborhood, built later as a low-cost housing development for Gunnery School personnel and their families.

Carole Lombard

On a cold January night in Las Vegas, Captain Wayne Williams lifted his DC-3 off the runway at the Western Air Express airport northeast of town and pointed it toward Burbank. The plane was heavily loaded, carrying fifteen soldiers, four civilian passengers and a crew of three. A few minutes later, a loud explosion was heard

throughout Las Vegas Valley; residents at Blue Diamond and Goodsprings saw towering sheets of fire erupt near the top of Mount Potosi southwest of Las Vegas.

It was dawn before searchers, among them many of Las Vegas' most prominent citizens, risked the treacherous and snowy climb up Potosi. By 9 a.m. it was apparent that there were no survivors. Among the victims was actress Carole Lombard, the wife of screen idol Clark Gable. It was January 17, 1942.

Gable was a familiar figure in Las Vegas. An avid sportsman, he often hunted in southern Utah, usually stopping over in the "best town by a damsite." He had received a Las Vegas divorce in 1939 and married Lombard a few days later. Hearing of the crash, he flew immediately to Las Vegas, arriving after midnight. Discouraged from joining the search parties, he paced his bungalow at the El Rancho Hotel. It was there that he received the telegram from Goodsprings, "No survivors — all killed instantly."

Why did the crash occur on a crystal clear night? For long after-

the whistle blew. The proprietor of Bill's Cabins on Clark Avenue promised to give a crack on the head to anyone who warned him to turn off his lights. Generally, the darkness caused Las Vegans only

The January 17, 1942 Review-Journal *brought news of Carole Lombard's death to Las Vegans.*

Women serving coffee and doughnuts to soldiers at the Las Vegas USO in 1943. (Florence Lee Jones Cahlan, second from right.)

ward, there were rumors of sabotage and stories concerning the sometimes erratic behavior of the pilot. Some blamed last minute changes in flight plans. After an extensive investigation the FBI closed the file. A Congressional committee and the Civil Aeronautics Board had the final word, "extreme pilot error."

[**1900**]   [**1930**]   [**1940**]

CIVIL WAR   1898 SPANISH – AMERICAN WAR   THE GREAT DEPRESSION   1941—1945 US IN WORLD WAR II
1861—1865   1941 PEARL HARBOR ATTACKED
                  1914–1919
                  WORLD WAR I

1865
The Civil War ends at Appomattox with General Lee's surrender.

1876
Custer's 7th Cavalry are killed by the Sioux at the Little Bighorn.

1898
Teddy Roosevelt charges up San Juan Hill in the Spanish-American War.

1915
RMS Lusitania is torpedoed by a German submarine and sinks off the coast of Ireland.

1917
The U.S. drafts 2.8 million American men and enters WWI.

1919
Treaty of Versailles ends WWI. French Marshall Foch reacted to the poorly designed treaty saying, "This is not peace. It is an Armistice for 20 years."

1941
Japanese attack Pearl Harbor with 183 aircraft in the first wave. 2,403 U.S. dead, 1,178 wounded, 21 ships sunk or damaged. The U.S. declares war on Japan.

1942
Army Air Force Gunnery School in Las Vegas graduates its first class of gunnery cadets.

Carole Lombard's plane goes down killing all aboard.

Hitler declares war on the U.S. and America enters WWII.

The Manhattan Project begins the Atomic age.

1944
June 6, D-Day marks the beginning of the end of WWII in Europe. Allied troops storm the beaches of Normandy.

GI Bill helps American Veterans attend college, or get vocational training, and obtain low interest home mortgages.

William Nellis

Throughout World War II, Las Vegas newspapers regularly kept the home front informed about the activities of Clark County men and women in military service. In September 1944, the *Evening Review-Journal* reprinted a long letter from a P-47 pilot with the 513th Fighter Squadron in Europe. In the letter to his father-in-law in Las Vegas, the young lieutenant described in harrowing detail his experience bailing out of his crippled Thunderbolt over France, and his rescue by a French farmer. The following January, the newspaper featured the airman's picture on the occasion of his promotion to first lieutenant. The article noted that he had grown up in Searchlight, Nevada and had starred in football for the Las Vegas High School Wildcats. He was quoted as looking forward to the completion of fifty more missions and a well-earned furlough. The lieutenant's name was William H. Nellis.

The poignancy of the article only became apparent two weeks later. The newspaper noted briefly

Lieutenant William H. Nellis poses with his Air Force Thunderbolt during the war. In 1950 the Las Vegas Army Airfield was renamed in his honor.

1945
First atomic explosion with the Trinity test in central New Mexico.

"Little Boy" the first of two atomic bombs is dropped over Hiroshima, Japan. Three days later a second bomb hits Nagasaki. WWII ends.

President Franklin Delano Roosevelt dies in Warm Springs, Ga. Truman assumes the presidency.

1947
Aviator Howard Hughes flies the Hercules. The wooden seaplane is nicknamed the "Spruce Goose" by the press. The plane never flies again.

1948
Soviet blockade of West

Berlin prompts airlift of supplies by U.S. and Allies.

1951
First atomic bomb test at Nevada Proving Grounds. Forty-six years later, the government admits the fallout may have caused 75,000 cases of cancer.

1955
C-54 transport, en route to the Area 51 installation

on the dry Groom Lake bed, crashed into the west side of Mt. Charleston. Fourteen died.

1956
Nellis Air Force Base

home to the Thunderbirds, the Air Force aerobatic team.

1958
Nellis AFB jet collides with a United Airlines DC-7, west of Las Vegas, 49 die.

1961
East Germany erects the Berlin Wall.

1989
Berlin Wall is dismantled. East and West Berliners

travel freely between sides.

1990
Germany reunited.

2001
September 11, Al Quaeda terrorists fly two commercial jetliners into the Twin Towers in New York.

2003
President Bush declares war on Iraq.

that Lt. Nellis had been reported missing in December, just days before the announcement of his promotion. In April 1945, the Air Force confirmed that Lt. Nellis had been killed in action flying his third Thunderbolt over Belgium.

In 1949, the old Las Vegas Army Air Field (once the Las Vegas Army Gunnery School) was re-activated as Las Vegas Air Force Base. Its new mission, just in time for the Korean conflict, was the training of fighter pilots. In May 1950, 1500 local citizens gathered at the base to hear a dedication speech by Nevada Governor Vail Pittman. The key figure at the ceremony was nine-year-old Gerry Nellis, who unveiled a plaque paying tribute to his fighter pilot father and renaming the field Nellis Air Force Base in his honor.

The Atom Bomb

On January 27, 1951, an atomic bomb was dropped at Frenchman Flat at what was then the Nevada Proving Grounds. It was the first atomic test in the United States since the Trinity explosion at Alamogordo, New Mexico ushered in the Atomic Age in 1945.

The first atmospheric blast in Nevada, seen and felt as far away as northern Utah, left people unsettled. But Las Vegans quickly conquered their nervousness. Commentator Bob Considine noted that an early test caused barely a hitch in a craps dealer's motion. "Must have been a A-Bomb," the dealer said. "Place your bets — new shooter coming out." Fremont Street merchants turned the test to advantage. After one particularly violent shaking

had shattered a few windows, one businessman swept up the broken glass and displayed it in a barrel with the sign "A-Bomb Souvenirs — Free."

A typical atomic blast and mushroom cloud over the Nevada desert.

The town came to love the Bomb. The Chamber of Commerce distributed brochures notifying locals and tourists of upcoming blasts and indicating good vantage points for picnic viewing of the shots. Strip hotels featured "Miss Atomic Bomb" contests, and local hair stylists created the Atomic Hairdo in the shape of a mushroom cloud. Only for the brave was the Atomic Cocktail — equal parts vodka, brandy and champagne, with a hint of sherry.

Downwinders in Nevada and Utah had much less reason to love the Bomb; they showed abnormally high incidence of cancer. There have, of course, been no atmospheric tests at the Site since the Limited Nuclear Test Ban Treaty of 1963 and no tests at all in the last few years. The present test moratorium, recently joined by France as well, takes some of the horror out of the thoughts of physicist Robert Oppenheimer at Alamogordo. At the moment of the Trinity test, Oppenheimer recalled words from the *Bhagavad Gita*: "I am become Death — the Shatterer of Worlds."

A 1952 test at the Nevada Test Site produced this mushroom cloud.

These mannequins are posed in Las Vegas on their way to the Nevada Test Site, where they will be part of an above-ground atomic test.

Chapter ELEVEN

The Strip

In the Beginning

In 1905, railroad baron William A. Clark envisioned his new town of Las Vegas as a community of sober, industrious blue-collar workers and Main Street merchants. The imbibing of intoxicating beverages was to be confined to a single block of First Street, and gambling, what there was of it, was conducted in smoky saloon back rooms. It didn't turn out according to Clark's plan, even at the beginning. Ingenious operators exploited loopholes in the restrictive deeds of sale to open saloons on Fremont Street, and small-time gamblers flouted the state's feeble legal efforts at limiting their livelihood. Yet for a quarter of a century, Las Vegas had nothing that could reasonably be called a gambling resort.

In December 1928, the town woke up with a start. President Coolidge signed a bill authorizing the construction, on the Colorado River near Las Vegas, of the giant public work which would be called, at various times, the Black Canyon Project, Boulder Dam, and Hoover Dam. Real estate agents, developers, and dealmakers began to fill the few hotel rooms in town. Houses were demolished to make room for office blocks, and rumors abounded of numerous large hotels to come. These soon foundered on the shoals of the Great Depression. It was the great dam itself that was soon to show Las Vegas the way.

The construction between 1931 and 1935 was a transforming moment for the city. It certainly helped that casino-style gambling was again permitted, beginning in 1931.

Perhaps the dam's most important contribution was to demonstrate to Las Vegas that the city's future lay in tourism. In 1932, the first full year of construction, 200,000 people visited Las Vegas and half of them made the pilgrimage to Black Canyon to watch high scalers and blasting crews at work. In 1934, the figure was over a quarter of a million. One of those visitors, English writer and dramatist J.B. Priestly, tried to sum up his feelings upon seeing the awesome project: "It is like the beginning of a new world," he said. "A world of giant machines and titanic communal enterprises."

But the construction period was fleeting. The tourist influx didn't lead to the building of resort hotels, though the elegant new Apache on Fremont Street and the modern Boulder Dam Hotel in Boulder City attracted their share of Hollywood stars. After 1935, the Great Depression caught up with Las Vegas, but the giant dam and Lake forming behind it continued to provide needed tourist income. For the moment, town boosters were content with advertising Las Vegas as the "gateway to Boulder Dam," but the experience had taught community leaders that the future lay in tourism.

Before there were "Spice Girls" there were "Dice Girls." The George Moro Dancers appeared at the El Rancho in the 1950s.

A parade on Fremont Street celebrates the signing of the Boulder Dam legislation in 1928.

The Frontiers

"What's in a name?" asks Shakespeare's Juliet. Well, quite a bit, if the name is "Frontier" and it's in Las Vegas. The city first consciously deployed the term in 1939 when it created a slogan for itself: "Still a Frontier Town." The concept was more than a bit anachronistic. Las Vegas was born in 1905. That was 15 years after the 1890 census disclosed that America no longer had a frontier. The first actual establishment of any consequence to bear that name was the Frontier Club on Fremont Street, opened by California gambler Guy McAfee in early 1939. While that club was successful, eventually being folded into McAfee's Golden Nugget, the name "Frontier" is most associated with the Strip. The germ of the Last Frontier Hotel and Casino on the Strip was a 1930s-era speakeasy, restaurant and gambling club called the Pair-O-Dice. The taste and elegance of

the Pair-O-Dice was in stark contrast to the predominantly Western theme of the rest of Las Vegas. McAfee bought that establishment in 1939 and operated it fitfully as the 91 Club. Then McAfee sold the property to developer R.E. Griffith who, in 1942, incorporated it into his Hotel Last Frontier, the second resort on the emerging Strip.

By 1950, the Last Frontier was playing up the Old West theme with a vengeance. Beside it to the north, the Last Frontier Village evolved. Dedicated to the preservation of history, the village contained a jail, a Chinese Joss House, and a trading post, all buildings acquired from old Nevada towns. On the grounds were a museum, a rifle range, an antique gun collection and ancient railroad and fire fighting equipment.

The Last Frontier Village could be considered a direct forerunner of themed shopping malls like the Forum Shops at Caesars Palace and the Venetian's Grand Canal Shoppes. Say it's 1950 and you want to show up at a charity ball in the latest fashionable apparel from Elsa Schiaparelli or Lily Dache. Where do you go? Probably to Fanny Soss's new dress shop outlet at the Last Frontier Village. That would also be the spot to pick up that special hunting rifle, some fine maple furniture, and many other items. The centerpiece of the village was a new Gay 90's-style saloon and gambling hall called the Golden Slipper, though that would very soon become *Silver* Slipper.

By mid-1951, the nine-year-old Last Frontier Hotel and Casino was looking a bit down-at-the-heels. Owner Bill Moore announced a two-year renovation plan to liven up the place. The theme would still be Old West. That was about a month before he sold the property. Guy McAfee and Jake Kozloff of the Golden Nugget and Beldon Katleman of El Rancho Vegas Hotel and Casino paid five-and-a-half million.

Under the new regime, the Last Frontier would be an entertainment highlight of Las Vegas. Among the performers to appear there were Benny Goodman, Sammy Davis, Ronald Reagan, and Josephine Baker. Miss Baker earned a special niche in Las Vegas history by refusing to perform before a whites-only audience, forcing management to admit a few black patrons.

Success led to pipe dreams. In April 1954, Last Frontier owners charted a major new course. Construction began on an entirely new building between the aging resort and the Silver Slipper. The decor would be a complete reversal. The slogan "Early West in Modern Splendor" was scrapped, as was the name "Last Frontier." The theme was the space age and the operation would thenceforth be called the *New* Frontier.

That first step into space proved a giant one indeed. A botched opening in 1955 was just the beginning of years of legal and financial turmoil. Singing sensation Mario Lanza was signed to be the opening act at the New Frontier's Venus Room, but he fled at the last minute, leaving other Las Vegas Strip performers to fill the void.

It was all downhill from there. Key owners, including Jake Kozloff, couldn't get licensed by the Nevada Tax Commission. The Commission was particularly puzzled by one "owner" who sued to recover his interest in the hotel though it had never been officially revealed that he was in fact an owner. Million-dollar lawsuits flew back and forth through the late 1950s. Ger-

man munitions heiress and valley resident Vera Krupp tried her hand briefly before backing out and filing her own suit. Warren Bayley of the Hacienda Hotel purchased the New Frontier property and re-opened it in 1959. The next year, the Internal Revenue Service snatched all the cash at the New *and* the Last Frontiers for unpaid withholding and excise taxes.

By the mid-1960s, the situation must have seemed a bad dream, for the New Frontier was moved back to the original Frontier site after the demolition of the remnants of the Last Frontier. This move also entailed a new name — the Frontier. The move came just in time for the rapacious Howard Hughes to gobble it up, but that's a story in itself.

After a lengthy and bitter labor dispute in the 1990s, post-Hughes owners of the property decided that yet a new name was in order. They resurrected the name "New Frontier." Which brings us to the punch line toward which this essay has been moving: Is the present New Frontier indeed the last Frontier?

Thunderbird

In the last two decades of the twentieth century, the Las Vegas Strip moved inexorably southward. Early in the new millennium, the demolition of a defunct resort styling itself the El Rancho refocused attention on the partly fallow north end of the Strip. That El Rancho wasn't the original El Rancho Vegas Hotel of 1941, which stood on the west side of Las Vegas Boulevard at Sahara Avenue, marking the Strip's

The Thunderbird Hotel in the mid-1950s.

official northern entrance until it burned down in 1960. But the newer El Rancho, on the opposite side of the Strip and a little farther south, did have a rich and almost forgotten history of its own — as the Thunderbird.

Built in 1948, the Thunderbird was the fourth of the great Strip resorts, coming just after the more infamous Flamingo. Like its immediate predecessor, the architecture was mostly modern, confirming a permanent shift away from the wagon wheel and sourdough image of 1940s Las Vegas. Also like the

Flamingo, its entertainment was first rate. The great bands of Jimmy Dorsey and Count Basie played there, and comedian Henny Youngman regularly provided the laughs.

The Thunderbird never had the luster of, say, the Flamingo or the Sands, but its place in gaming history is secure. It inadvertently played a central role in creating the present gaming control mechanism in Nevada. In the 1950s, the hotel figured in a controversy over hidden underworld ownership.

Having discovered that Jake Lansky, brother of eastern gangster

Meyer Lansky, had made a substantial "loan" to the resort, the Nevada Tax Commission suspended its license in 1955. The hotel appealed to the Nevada Supreme Court. The scandal contributed to the creation in that year's legislative session of the more powerful Gaming Control Board. When the state's highest court finally handed down its opinion in the licensing case in 1957, it confirmed the power of the Board to suspend or revoke gaming licenses. Without this development, Nevada might not have been able to withstand persistent federal at-

The Dunes in 1955.

tempts to regulate gambling. That should have been sufficient cause to shed a figurative tear when the last remnant of the 1940s Strip came down.

Resorts 1955

The first florescence of the Las Vegas resort industry came in the early 1950s when the Desert Inn, Sahara, and Sands Hotels created desert oases along the Strip and the Showboat docked beside Boulder Highway. Nineteen fifty-five in particular, was expected to be spectacular. That year offers probably the closest historical parallel to the phenomenal growth of the 1990s. In April, three hotels opened on the Strip. The Last Frontier Ho-

tel inched northward with an apt new name: New Frontier. Farther north, the Royal Nevada opened a few days later featuring operatic star Helen Traubel.

The third hotel to debut that month was a dramatic departure. At nine stories, the Riviera towered over its Lilliputian neighbors, signaling that future growth on the Strip would be as much vertical as horizontal. The salary paid its opening performer was comparably grand. A young pianist, long known to local audiences as Walter Liberace, received a precedent-setting $50,000 per week for five weeks. The following month saw the opening of yet two more resorts. The Dunes, with its distinctive thirty-foot-high

fiberglass Sultan, opened on May 23. On May 24 the elegant Moulin Rouge, the only Las Vegas resort welcoming black patrons, opened on West Bonanza Road.

What was to be a banner year quickly turned to disaster, as all of the new resorts experienced financial difficulty. There were simply not enough patrons to go around. Problems with highly paid performers were only the tip of the iceberg. At the New Frontier, tenor Mario Lanza, claiming illness, missed the grand opening. Comic Wally Cox, television's "Mr. Peepers," bombed at the Dunes despite vociferous applause from friend Marlon Brando and his entourage. Older resorts stepped in to bail out the new entries as several hotels contributed headliners to replace Lanza, and the Sands briefly and none too successfully took over management of the Dunes casino.

Former Flamingo boss Gus Greenbaum, summoned out of retirement in Arizona, helped tide the Riviera over a drastic early slump. The Royal Nevada, unable to pay its bills, limped along for a time before declaring bankruptcy in January. No one helped the Moulin Rouge and it closed in October. The troubles of 1955 proved fleeting, but is it a cautionary tale about over-expansion?

The Sands

Watching the demolition of Las Vegas Strip landmarks has become part of the Las Vegas spectacle. After nearly forty-four years of operation, the Sands Hotel and Casino in 1996 followed the Landmark, the Dunes and original Flamingo into oblivion.

Not that anything about the Sands was routine. Producer Jack

The Sands in 1954.

Entratter's connections with media figures such as Louella Parsons, Earl Wilson, Hedda Hopper and Walter Winchell ensured that the Sands would always find its "place in the sun" as the hotel's motto proclaimed. Many of the more famous stories were retold — the coalescing of Sands headliners into the "Rat Pack" in 1959 during the filming of the movie *Ocean's Eleven,* and the one-sided fight in 1967 between Frank Sinatra and Sands executive Carl Cohen (Sinatra lost, and the Sands lost Sinatra).

One of the most effective Las Vegas promotions ever came in 1953 when Sands publicist Al Freeman had gambling tables lowered into the swimming pool. The resulting photograph of a "floating crap game" lured many to this bizarre place in the desert where one apparently could gamble even while taking a dip.

There are some lesser-known facts about the Sands. Few Las Vegans recall that it was Billy Wilkerson of

Hollywood, not Bugsy Siegel, who conceived the Flamingo Hotel. But even fewer know that the Sands grew out of yet another Wilkerson brainchild. In 1950, Wilkerson, owner of several Southern California nightspots, opened the elegant LaRue on the Las Vegas Strip. Two years later, the LaRue became the basis for the Sands.

The most notable part of the Sands complex, the circular tower, wasn't built until 1965. One of the most attractive buildings on the Strip, it was designed by architect Martin Stern, Jr. When the Sands was demolished, there was no lack of Stern buildings to see in Las Vegas. The prolific architect also designed Bally's; the Mint tower, which is now part of the Horseshoe; and parts of the present Flamingo and Sahara Hotels.

Hacienda

Would you sink money into a Las Vegas resort hotel if a respected national magazine hinted darkly on its cover that Las Vegas was about to crap out? Well, neither would a lot of other folks in 1955, and a new hotel project at the far south end of the Las Vegas Strip languished for lack of funds.

The unfinished hotel was the Lady Luck and it was trying to buck a trend that saw five resorts open that year and run immediately into financial difficulty. Not only that, but the Stardust, Tropicana, and Fremont were also racing toward completion. The man who saved the Lady Luck was Warren "Doc" Bayley, affiliated with a chain of California hotels operating under the name of Hacienda. The Lady Luck became the Hacienda.

Getting the resort open was still not easy. Jake Kozloff, who had been named casino boss, couldn't get licensing approval through the new Gaming Control Board because of certain prior irregularities. Locals suspected that, more than anything, the board wanted to put the brakes on runaway casino development in Southern Nevada. The Hacienda Hotel opened without a casino in June 1956. Under a new casino manager, the Hacienda finally got its license and began operation as a gaming resort that November.

The Hacienda was to add several new wrinkles to the timeworn Las Vegas promotion schemes. In 1957, construction on Highway 91 at Victorville, California required drivers to come to a full stop. At that point, a pretty cocktail waitress would hand the driver a coupon. Presented at the Hacienda with sixteen dollars, the coupon entitled the visitor to a room and ten dollars in hotel scrip, good for food, drink or gambling. Curiously, the Clark County liquor and gaming board frowned on this innovation as a "tourist trap."

The Hacienda is probably most noted for operating its own airline. At its peak, the Hacienda operated over thirty aircraft, flying passengers to and from the hotel without charge. The Civil Aeronautics Board, under pressure from commercial airlines, was not amused and, after a long battle, forced an end to the private airline.

Like several honored predecessors, the Hacienda eventually was imploded on national television, and Mandalay Bay now stands on the site. Fortunately, at least a piece of the Hacienda remains. Its gigantic neon sign, depicting a caballero on a rearing steed, now towers over Fremont Street as the first of many classic neon signs to be installed downtown by the Neon Museum.

Chapter TWELVE

Small Clubs

Arizona Club

Realtors like to say that the first three principles of their business are location, location and location. In 1905, J.O. McIntosh thought he had all three covered. At the May auction that started Las Vegas, McIntosh bought two choice lots on north First Street — two lots in the heart of Block 16. That and a neighboring block were the only areas in town where the sale of liquor was permitted. McIntosh built a false-fronted wood frame saloon he called the Arizona Club and began to sell the finest bourbons Kentucky had to offer. His gin fizzes became regionally famous.

So certain was he of the advantages of location that he applied to the First State Bank for a $60,000 loan to completely rebuild. That bank officers approved the loan was to him an assurance that that the liquor prohibition in the rest of the townsite would hold up. He built a truly elegant establishment with

The Arizona Club around the time of the opening of its new building in 1906. The original establishment opened in 1905.

beveled glass windows from France, pink Tennessee marble baseboards, and a massive oak bar.

His grand opening on March 31, 1906 was a noteworthy event. Ladies, not normally welcome in this gentleman's environment, were extended a special invitation. White-uniformed bartenders served champagne brunch, as an orchestra played classical music.

That was about the time that Fremont Street property owners found legal loopholes in the prohibition clauses. McIntosh promptly sold out. Later proprietors added a second floor and a new line of commerce — prostitution — and the saloon began to blend in to the general seaminess of Block 16. But for a time, the Arizona Club had been the most elegant drinking establishment in Southern Nevada.

The elegant interior of the Arizona Club. Ladies were not welcome here except by invitation.

The Moulin Rouge

The resort hotels that opened in Las Vegas in the 1950s had more than their desert themes in common. In a time of deepening segregation in Las Vegas, they were closed to African-Americans. Even nationally prominent black entertainers could not mingle with guests in the public areas. Often they were not permitted to stay at the hotels and had to seek accommodations on the predominantly black Westside of Las Vegas.

The exception was the Moulin Rouge on West Bonanza Road. Opened in May 1955, the Moulin Rouge was Las Vegas' first interracial resort. Prominent black figures occupied key positions. Clarence Robinson, veteran producer of shows in New York, London and at the original Moulin Rouge in Paris, put together the first floor show. Sonnny Boswell, the former Harlem Globetrotters basketball star who also had managed a Chicago hotel, accepted the same job at the Moulin Rouge, and former heavyweight boxing champion Joe Louis served as host. Blacks worked as dealers, security guards and cocktail waitresses, positions denied to them elsewhere.

A "Who's Who" of Hollywood and New York celebrities, black and white, joined the packed audiences in the posh Cafe Rouge showroom. Entertainers there included jazz legends Benny Carter and Lionel Hampton, as well as Dinah Washington, bandleader Les Brown and nine-year-old dancer Gregory Hines. The casino lounge featured jazz artists Wild Bill Davis and Ahmad Jamal, as well as the Platters and the Penguins, who appeared before their songs *The Great Pretender* and *Earth Angel* hit the top of the pop charts.

The hotel closed after only five months. The full story of its closure will likely never be known. Claims of insufficient capitalization and mismanagement were countered by charges that Strip operators tried to prevent their employees from patronizing the Moulin Rouge and urged creditors to bring suit for payment of overdue bills. In the latter theory, the downfall of the Moulin Rouge was hastened by its success. Its 2:30 a.m. late show attracted droves of gamblers and celebrities away from the Strip. At a time when the Strip resorts were helping one another to avert mutual catastrophe, there were no offers of support for the Moulin Rouge.

Racial barriers on the Strip finally fell five years later. For its role in helping to bring that about, the Moulin Rouge was listed on the National Register of Historic Places and was declared an historic landmark by the City of Las Vegas. Tragically, like so many of the city's historic treasures, the Moulin Rouge was destroyed by fire in 2003, as its newest owners made plans to renovate and reopen.

The Green Shack

American Heritage Dictionary defines an institution as a "custom, practice, relationship or behavioral pattern of importance in the life of a community . . ." The Green Shack was an institution.

The 1930s restaurant wasn't just another of the many Boulder Highway roadhouses which dished up food, entertainment and raw whiskey to thousands of dam workers. It provided a comfortable and egalitarian environment for families, high school graduation parties, and civic meetings. Local lore has it that Ben Siegel frequented the place in the 1940s. Why not? Everyone else did. The Green Shack was an informal resort association, chamber of commerce, city hall and courthouse, where deals

The Moulin Rouge dancers performed the "Can-Can" routine, and audiences packed the house.

The Green Shack was the unimposing place to be seen for Las Vegas movers, shakers, and rounders.

were made and cases settled over congenial libations.

The Green Shack was the creation of Mrs. Jimmie Jones, who came to Las Vegas in 1929 following the death of her husband. Her first place, called the Colorado, was situated where Fremont Street then petered out into a dirt trail. It offered fried chicken and bootleg whiskey through a window in her home. When the road was realigned to accommodate construction traffic, Mrs. Jones bought a green barracks building from the railroad and hauled it to a spot beside the new highway. The color and character of the building suggested its name.

The end of Prohibition permitted the addition of a cocktail lounge and gambling in 1934, and nephew Frank McCormick, father of the last owner to run the restaurant,

managed that part of the operation. The place hasn't changed greatly since then. Of late, the Green Shack served as a respite from high speed modern Las Vegas. To enter it was to shed decades. No more. The McCormicks have hung up their skillets. Las Vegas, it seems, has lost an institution, another link with its past.

Jackson Street

Mention Fremont Street or the Las Vegas Strip almost anywhere in the world and people will recognize them instantly. A third Las Vegas street was also widely known for a time, but mainly among entertainers and some local residents. To them, Jackson Street rivaled the other two for the quality of its nightlife.

It's not surprising that more people were not familiar with it, since Jackson Street is on the pre-

dominantly black Westside. Prone as always to sensationalism and fascination with crime, the press in the 1940s and 1950s tended to report only the occasional brawl and license violation associated with Westside clubs.

The clubs began to open in the war years of the early 1940s, as new black residents swelled the population of the Westside. The Brown Derby, the Harlem Club and the Cotton Club provided opportunities for entertainment and nightlife. They were destinations too for black soldiers on leave from the nearby military bases. In a segregated environment, these soldiers were denied entrance to all clubs but those on the Westside. There were unfortunate incidents. The most serious happened in January 1944 when fifty parched soldiers from Camp Clipper in the Mojave

Desert descended on the tiny Brown Derby. The inevitable spark touched off a brawl, which brought in the Las Vegas police. One soldier was killed by a police officer, and the area was off-limits to the military for a time.

In the mid-1950s, Jackson Street became an alternative center of gambling and first-rate jazz, blues and popular entertainment. A hotel to be called the Moulin Rouge began construction in 1954 and, after some difficulty, opened as the Carver House at D and Jackson. The new Moulin Rouge opened not far away, on Bonanza Road, and stimulated the opening of clubs like the El Morocco and Louisiana.

Headlining performers downtown and on the Strip were unable to frequent the hotels where they performed. Pearl Bailey, Lena Horne, Sammy Davis, Jr. and others brought celebrity audiences with them to the Westside. On any morning from 2 a.m. to noon, Jackson Street was the place to be. Ironically, the very success of civil rights efforts in the 1950s and 1960s, which opened doors on the East side, led to a withering of Westside night life. Westside residents are still looking forward to the economic development, which will bring a resurgence to their community.

Monte Carlo

After the glittering opening of the new Monte Carlo, the newspaper gushed over its opulence. An article noted the crystal chandelier and the luxury decor of the cocktail bar and opined that it was probably the most elaborate space in all America. No, it wasn't 1996 or about a casino opening on the Las Vegas Strip; it was 1945 and the Monte Carlo Casino was located on Fremont Street, at the historic site of the old Northern Club, which had ob-

Souvenir postcard of the Monte Carlo Casino.

tained Clark County's first gaming license in 1931.

The Monte Carlo was the creation of Wilbur Clark, a veteran of Southern California's offshore gambling boats. Clark had begun his Las Vegas career in 1944 by purchasing a chunk of the El Rancho Vegas Hotel. The Monte Carlo was but another stepping stone to his most notable achievement. This was the opening and operating, in a junior partnership role with Cleveland's Moe Dalitz, of the Desert Inn Hotel and Casino. Clark, in fact, operated the Monte Carlo for only a few months before moving on.

Given the luster and prestige of the name "Monte Carlo" in gambling circles, it's not surprising that the name has even deeper roots in Las Vegas. In March 1931, a man by the name of Roy Grimes was among the first applicants for a city gaming license after the statewide legalization of gambling that month. Having leased a part of David Lorenzi's rural resort northwest of town, Grimes wanted to operate a craps table.

The city council, having determined to limit gaming establishments, refused to grant a license to Grimes. Arguing that the city had acted capriciously, Grimes urged the commission to reverse its decision, but a majority of the board refused. Grimes sued the city, and in early May the case went before the Nevada Supreme Court. On July 8, 1931, the Supreme Court handed down an important decision upholding the right of municipalities to limit gaming licenses. Apparently feeling vindicated, the city granted Grimes a license the following week. This first Monte Carlo Casino operated only very briefly, but it had inadvertently established an important legal principle.

Seven Thieves

The area where Fremont, Charleston and Boulder Highway come together was one hell-raising neighborhood in 1931. It was a Depression year, but Las Vegas was having an exhilarating time. Gamblers could again operate legally, and with Boulder Dam construction just starting, there were lots of paychecks to be wagered. But Prohibition was still in effect, and Las Vegas' beckoning proximity to tee-totaling Boulder City made it a prime target of federal antiliquor agents. They had their work cut out for them. Gin mills sprouted near the Boulder Dam Highway like roadside weeds.

Most of the new places were as ephemeral as the foam on their bootleg beer. One that survived for a time was a resort called the Meadows. Swanky by local standards, it was a favorite hangout for bar crawlers. After the dam was completed, the Meadows limped along until a fire conveniently put it out of business in 1943. Nearby, on the curve of Boulder Highway, the Green Shack building, although no

longer a restaurant, remained as of 2005 a reminder of that era.

Amazingly, another of that cluster of 1930s roadhouses is still there. The Den of Seven Thieves opened at Charleston Boulevard and 25th Street in August 1931. A month later, prohibition agents closed it down. A similar fate befell its successor, the Black Cat Inn. Then came a long series of ownership and name changes. As the Kit Kat Club in 1942 it showcased exotic dancers for the edification of Henderson's defense workers. It must have been a spirit of friendly competition that led a gang of these patrons to march across the street and tear up the plush Colony Club, disrupting the show of famed bubble dancer Sally Rand.

Shortly thereafter new owners renamed it the Saddle Club. Most longtime Las Vegans will remember it in a still later incarnation as the Silver Dollar Saloon, for over three decades a top spot for country music and dancing. With its new incarnation as the Silver Saddle Saloon, it's given the intersection a spark of its former excitement. It may be a bit glitzier than the original Den of Seven Thieves, but with a little imagination you can still picture a gang of dam workers stopping in to slake a mighty thirst.

The Big Four Club and Venetian Ballroom

On the main thoroughfares of Las Vegas, most of the buildings which might remind us of the city's past have vanished or are disguised by vast neon displays. The side streets, though, sometimes offer surprising

revelations about earlier times. On First Street, for example, just south of Fremont, there is an old, fairly nondescript two-story building. The most recent occupant, LeRoy's Horse and Sports Place, was itself something of a throwback to a pre-resort city time. The building's earliest incarnations are a part of Prohibition- and Depression-era Las Vegas.

Built in 1931 for local banker and businessman Leland Ronnow, the building was to house two commercial establishments on the ground floor, and a laundry did operate there briefly. The second floor became the Venetian Ballroom. Opened in September 1931 by three Californians, the Venetian promised a seven-piece orchestra, dance instructors, and an environment in which the most fastidious could enjoy themselves. Admission to the ballroom was ten cents, and gentlemen paid five cents a dance or seventy-five cents for an entire evening of dancing with the ballroom hostesses.

Advertising for "fountain refreshments" was, of course, code for "bring a hip flask." The police didn't look kindly on this illegal practice and closed the place up shortly after it opened. With a promise to police itself more carefully, the Venetian soon reopened and for the next several years served as an affordable nightspot. It was also headquarters for the new local chapter of the American Federation of Musicians and a spot for members to jam and hold benefit dances.

The first floor of the building also has a history. Nevada legalized gambling in late March 1931. On April 1, the county commission granted the first four gambling licenses. One of them was to the Big Four Club, which promptly opened in the Ronnow Building. The Big Four also quickly ran into difficulty with the cops. After several years of periodic closings and re-openings, new management explained the reason in 1937.

The Big Four had gotten an unsavory reputation by serving as friendly headquarters for the unemployed seeking work in Southern Nevada, and for the labor leaders who tried to help them. For the working stiffs who were successful, the Big Four became their hangout. It wasn't enough; the Big Four went under before the end of the decade. Somehow this relic of a fascinating past has escaped the wrecking ball.

The Biltmore

Some of Nevada's once-famous resorts go out with a bang, and some with a whimper. Millions watched national TV coverage of the Sands Hotel implosion in 1996. Almost no one noticed the destruction by fire of the building, which was once the Nevada Biltmore Hotel.

The Nevada Biltmore project was announced in December 1930 by a Hollywood investment firm. It was to be a tourist hotel catering to visitors in town to gawk at Boulder Dam as well as a haven for wealthy Californians wishing to undo the bonds of matrimony. Its proposed location was not immediately revealed. It wasn't revealed, in fact, for twelve years.

The Nevada Biltmore finally opened in 1942 at the corner of Main Street and Bonanza Road. Owner Bob Brooks of Beverly Hills had created a South Seas-themed resort. Patrons could listen to Hawaiian music and sip on exotic rum drinks amid decor that included a surfboard once belonging to famed surfer Duke Kahanamoku. Topnotch floorshows were packed nightly.

In September 1944, Brooks announced that the financially ailing resort was not for sale. Three months later, he sold it to southern California developer G.E. Kensey. Despite an expansion a year later, Kensey had to eliminate the floorshows to save money. Bandleader and radio personality Horace Heidt took over the property in 1946 and managed it for about a year. His show business connections were instrumental in bringing in acts like Francis Faye, exotic dancer Sally Rand, and the internationally acclaimed Mills Brothers.

The Biltmore reached its apogee during 1947. Under the management of Detroit nightclub owner Frank Barbaro, the resort showcased comedians like Chico Marx, Ben Blue, and Martha Raye. The financial effort exhausted the operation, which closed while owners and lessees battled in court. In 1949, a Dallas company bought the lease and for a very brief time operated it as a resort for black patrons. That idea was ahead of its time. Under still new owners, the property changed to the Shamrock Hotel, which hung on for a time. As the century drew to a close, the once-exciting complex was reduced to a furniture store and blue-collar tavern, before a fire ended its history and the remains were bulldozed.

The Nevada Biltmore Hotel and the daily poolside beauty parade.

Las Vegas Club

The Las Vegas Club on Main and Fremont is not always accorded its due as one of the oldest hotel/casinos on Fremont Street. It's time to remedy that oversight.

The original Las Vegas Hotel, *not* a direct ancestor of the present one, was opened just before the 1905 land auction which gave birth to the city of Las Vegas. That board and canvas hostelry on north Main Street provided rough accommodations to business travelers for some months after the auction.

The present Las Vegas Club Hotel and Casino, while not the first, is still a venerable establishment by Las Vegas standards. It has its roots in 1908 when John Horden and Harry Beale built their new Las Vegas Club hotel on the south side of Fremont, between Main and First Streets. (It's worth noting that Harry Beale had previously operated Las Vegas' first resort, a tent restaurant and dance floor at the Old Las Vegas Ranch in 1905.)

The Las Vegas Club's 1908 opening date confers on it a strong claim to be the oldest casino in Las Vegas continuously doing business under the same name. Its gambling tradition extends back even before the state of Nevada made all forms of gambling illegal in 1910. When legal gambling returned in 1931,

the Las Vegas Club received one of the first five licenses granted by Clark County. The current Golden Gate Hotel, built in 1906 as the Hotel Nevada, is an older hotel, but there was no gambling there until 1955. (In 1931 the Hotel Nevada became the Sal Sagev, Las Vegas spelled backward; in 1955

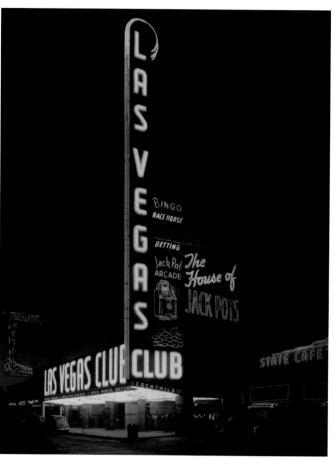

The Las Vegas Club in the 1940s.

its first floor became the Golden Gate Casino.)

The Las Vegas Club also has the distinction of having been operated by a "Who's Who?" of major Las Vegas gambling figures. Shortly after the re-legalization of gambling in 1931, Kell Houssells took over operation. Houssells' career took an upward curve from there as he

went on to acquire the El Cortez and, later, the Tropicana. In 1945, he announced a new management team at the Las Vegas Club, consisting of Moe Sedway and Gus Greenbaum, later of the Flamingo, Riviera and other resorts.

In the late 1940s, Texas gambler Benny Binion entered into a partnership with Houssells, until the latter decided to move the Las Vegas Club across the street to its present location on the northeast corner of Main and Fremont, and merge it with the Overland Hotel. (The original wooden Overland, constructed in 1906, burned and was rebuilt in concrete in 1911.) Meanwhile, Binion converted the Las Vegas Club building into the Westerner Club, before moving across the street to open the Eldorado Club in the Apache Hotel (which evolved into the Horseshoe Hotel and Casino in 1951.)

Beale and Horden's old Mission-style 1908 structure, which started as the Las Vegas Club and metamorphosed into the Westerner, is still there in its original location, enveloped in the Pioneer Club with its beckoning-cowboy sign, one of Las Vegas' most famous. It still has the name and the sign even though the casino has been converted to a gift shop.

Chapter THIRTEEN

Characters

Baby Face Nelson

In the 1930s, the *Las Vegas Evening Review-Journal* was reticent about revealing that there were Las Vegans with underworld connections. The *Review-Journal's* editor, Al Cahlan, made a curious exception to the rule in January 1936. Cahlan recalled speculation in 1934 that "Public Enemy Number One," Baby Face Nelson, had stayed for a time in Las Vegas.

Now, Cahlan said, it was established fact that Nelson had actually resided here for some time. He had stayed at an auto court on Fifth Street near Charleston Boulevard. Cahlan described his informant as "a young man who has been here several years, knows all the ins and outs, and is still amongst us." The young man, he also said, had underworld contacts.

Las Vegas resident John Detra may have shed some light on Baby Face Nelson in Las Vegas and where else he could have stayed. Detra's

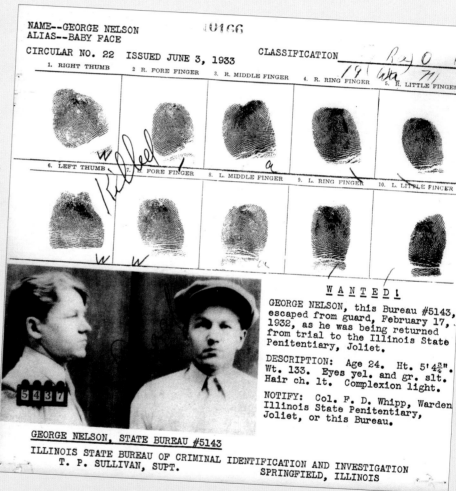

father, Frank Detra, owned the Pair-O-Dice Casino and restaurant on what is now the Las Vegas Strip. Next to the nightclub was a small outbuilding, perhaps fourteen-by-fourteen feet. They called it the "monkey house" because of a scheme to use monkeys in a gambling game

similar to "mouse roulette," offered for a time in Reno. The primates had been housed briefly in the small building.

Detra Junior also recalls the building being used as a hideaway on two or three occasions. Just a small boy at the time, he sat in the monkey house on the lap of a man he remembered as either "Pretty Boy" Floyd or "Baby Face" Nelson. It wasn't Floyd, who was having his own hideaway problems in Oklahoma. Perhaps, Frank Detra, who had lived in Chicago and knew Al Capone, was the young man who "knew the ins and outs." Whatever the case, it appears likely that Las Vegas was indeed the last home of "Baby Face" Nelson, just weeks before he was gunned down by federal agents in Illinois.

A. Lacey Worswick

Architect A. Lacey Worswick had already achieved much before his arrival in Las Vegas in 1929. He designed numerous buildings in San Francisco in the aftermath of the earthquake and fire of 1906. According to Las Vegas newspapers, he became chief of that city's bureau of architecture in 1912.

In Las Vegas, he picked up where he had left off in California. Soon after his arrival, he designed a beautiful residence for Southern Nevada businessman S.R. Whitehead on North Seventh Street. Converted to professional use, that home was placed on the National Register of Historic Places. The listing recognized its architectural significance and the importance of its original owner. Unfortunately, the building was destroyed in a fire after having been donated to the Junior League of Las Vegas, and moved to a temporary location.

In September 1931, Worswick was a busy man. Not only was he supervising final construction of the Apache Hotel, the building which can be glimpsed behind the enveloping signs of the Horseshoe Club, but he was also overseeing construction of a remarkable building at the corner of Eighth and Ogden. This was the modern new Las Vegas Hospital, a massive Mission Revival building of gypsite adobe bricks. This building, in which an entire generation of Las Vegans was born, burned to the ground in 1988 after being boarded up for several years.

Over the next two decades, Worswick designed an astonishing array of buildings, including offices, schools, a supermarket, a movie theater, a bank, many residences, and even a South Seas- style cocktail lounge. Much that is worth preserving of the Las Vegas of the rapid growth years of Hoover Dam and World War II is attributable to this single, amazingly energetic architect.

Leigh Hunt

The war years of 1941 to 1945 were a time of explosive population growth in Las Vegas Valley. On the edge of town south of Charleston Boulevard, one of the new housing tracts bore the name "Huntridge." The "Hunt" in Huntridge referred to Leigh S.J. Hunt, one of the most widely traveled and accomplished Las Vegas residents ever.

Few locals were aware of Leigh Hunt's varied background. Born in Indiana in 1855, he became an educator, and president of the college that was to become Iowa State University. Seeking his fortune later on the Pacific Slope, he migrated to Seattle where he took over the *Post-Intelligencer* newspaper and became a power in industry, real estate, and politics. Some said that he arrived in the city on Friday and took over its government on Saturday.

Wiped out in the Panic of 1893, he went to Korea, where the unstable politics of the era foiled a promising gold mining venture. Hunt's wanderings took him next to Africa. His timing in the Sudan was better. Working with a London syndicate, he helped improve the irrigation system and introduced there the profitable cultivation of long-staple cotton. During these years he counted among his friends and associates such notables as Mark Twain, William Dean Howells, Theodore Roosevelt and Booker T. Washington.

Opportunities for gypsum mining and a healthful climate drew Hunt and his family to Las Vegas in 1924 for what he called his "last good punch." He also predicted that, if the hoped-for dam project on the Colorado River became a reality, Las Vegas would become the great resort center of the Southwest.

Operating quietly, he purchased vast tracts of desert land south of town. Two years after his arrival, he planned a first-class resort hotel. That project foundered on the widespread belief among potential investors that a tourist hotel, a mile and a half from Fremont Street, just wouldn't work. Leigh Hunt died in 1933, far too early to see the metropolis of his dreams. It would have pleased him enormously to know that much of the Las Vegas Strip was later built on his land.

Boulder Dam Project
The Progress of this Vast Engineering Work is Fully and Accurately Covered. Associated Press and United Press Wire Service Bring News of the World to This Paper—A Leader For More Than A Quarter Of A Century.

LAS VEGAS AGE
SOUTHERN NEVADA'S LEADING NEWSPAPER

VOL. XXVII.   LAS VEGAS, CLARK COUNTY, NEVADA, THURSDAY MORNING, MARCH 26, 1931   No. 37

LAS VEGAS WEATHER
March 24—Maximum, 71; minimum, 42.
March 25—Maximum, 70; minimum, 42.

METAL MARKET
NEW YORK, March 25, (I.P)—Lead unchanged at 4.50 New York and 4.35 St. Louis. Zinc unchanged at 4.00 E. St. Louis.

"WHISKEY PETE" SHOOTS MAN
Woman, 4 Men Arrested In Insurance Fraud

ARREST FIVE IN HUGE L. A. FRAUD CASE

Wife of Louis Frank, Gangster, One of Quintette

LOS ANGELES, March 25, (I.P)—Four men and a woman accused of selling $3,000,000 in fraudulent insurance to large corporations in

ILLINOIS TO KILL STATE

WILBUR DENIES HE'S TO RESIGN

ABOARD U. S. S. ARIZONA, AT SEA, March 25 (I.P)—It was authoritatively stated tonight that Ray Lyman Wilbur has no intention of retiring as Secretary of Interior, as reported in Washington and Denver. Wilbur is accompanying President Hoover on his vacation trip.

SEC. WILBUR IS EXPECTED TO RESIGN

Denver Attorney Is Thought Possible Successor

DENVER, March 25 (I.P) — The Denver Post said today that advices from Washington indicate that Wil-

Boulder City Furnishes Its First Marriage

Boulder City contracted its first couple for the marriage vows yesterday when Rev. C. H. Reynolds performed the ceremony at the M. E. parsonage which united Ray E. Rutherford, 21, and Isle Phillips, 16. Consent to the marriage was given before the bound clerk when the license was issued by Myrtle

BIDS OPENED FOR HIGHWAY IMPROVEMENT

Isbell Bros. Low Bidders on Two North-South Projects

CARSON CITY, March 25, (Special)—Bids were opened here this

WINTER IN ITS DEATH THROES IN MOUNTAINS

Wyoming and Montana Scenes of Violent Storms

DENVER, March 25, (I.P)—A blizzard gathered momentum on the

MAN HURT BADLY IN COLLISION

Traveling at a high rate of speed, two cars came together, head-on on the highway near Erie shortly after two-thirty this morning. A man giving his name as Joe W. Amos, living at 2050 Victoria Ave., Los Angeles was the most seriously injured. Amos was rushed to the Ferguson-Bolomo Hospital by passing motorists. He is suffering from

POSTMASTER AT ELGIN IS SHOT IN ARM

Bradshaw Shot Down As He Reaches For Paper

"Whiskey Pete"

Pete McIntyre was no stranger to the inside of a courtroom. On one occasion, in 1931, the charge was assault with a deadly weapon. In an incident at Pete's service station near the California border south of Las Vegas, Pete had shot Rube Bradshaw in the arm and side. The men naturally had different versions of the incident. The charge was eventually dropped; Bradshaw was in a Utah hospital and unavailable for testimony.

Pete had earlier served six months in connection with some bootleg whiskey confiscated by police in his absence. It is a measure of the man's tenacity that Pete immediately hopped freight to Las Vegas, stormed into the sheriff's office, and demanded the return of his property. The sheriff, lacking humor, clapped him in jail. Perhaps it was this incident that earned him the nickname "Whiskey Pete."

Pete was generous to his friends but short tempered with motorists who stopped at his station for free water and no gas. With his handy .45 and excellent booze, he became a legend in Las Vegas, a town just beginning to cultivate a Wild West image.

Pete died in 1933. His long-expressed wish had been to be buried upright with a bottle of whiskey in his hand. Witnesses attest that he was laid to rest at least at such an angle that the bottle kept sliding from his hand and had to be tucked into his belt. A few years back, while excavating for expansion, workers for the resort casino that now stands at the site uncovered a coffin with human remains. Was it Pete? There was no bottle to be found nearby.

"Colonel" Bob Russell

When construction began on Boulder Dam in 1931, Las Vegas was wide open for enterprising businessmen. One, Los Angeles hotel man Robert R. Russell, snapped up the chance to lease the new hotel at the corner of Second and Fremont. Now the older section of Binion's Horseshoe, it opened in 1932 as the Apache, Las Vegas' largest and most elegant hotel.

Russell soon assumed leadership of the Chamber of Commerce and became the city's most tireless and effective promoter. Not that much promotion was needed at first. The enormous construction project in Black Canyon was advertisement enough, drawing hundreds of thousands of awed sightseers. Most of them had to stay in Las Vegas.

At first there was nothing particularly unusual about Russell. Gradually, though, the courtly, college-educated hotel proprietor evolved into "Colonel" Bob Russell, the self-avowed biggest liar in Nevada. With his western garb, long, flowing hair, handlebar moustache and goatee, he became the spitting image of Buffalo Bill Cody. He enchanted tourists with his tall tales of the Old West.

His skills as a publicist were desperately needed after 1935. Construction on the dam was complete, Southern Nevada's population was dwindling, and once-booming Las Vegas began settling into the slough of the Great Depression. It was at this point that the Las Vegas Chamber adopted the slogan "Still

a Frontier Town" and created the annual Old West celebration of Helldorado.

Two of Russell's contributions helped bring Las Vegas to the attention of millions of potential visitors. He concocted a publicity story about a scruffy prospector who had just hit it big and came in for a night on the town. Conveniently, a Union Pacific photographer happened to catch a shot of the old sourdough registering himself and his burro for two rooms at the Apache. The pictures went out over the wires, and readers from coast to coast fell for the story.

The most famous Russell ploy was aimed at potential anglers. The same UP photographer captured Russell catching the first fish at Lake Mead. Only the most discerning would notice that the long, slender fish looked suspiciously like an ocean-dwelling barracuda. It had come to Lake Mead by way of a San Pedro fish market. A decade later, professional PR firms would devise slicker campaigns to promote Las Vegas, but the city owes a lot to Colonel Bob Russell for its early successes.

"Colonel" Bob Russell, the biggest liar in Nevada, and consummate publicist, far right.

Howard Hughes

In the pre-dawn hours of November 27, 1966, just three days after Thanksgiving, a special train stopped at a remote junction north of Las Vegas. Unseen except by his closest aides, Howard Hughes transferred to a van which whisked him to the Desert Inn Hotel. For the next four years, he never left his penthouse suite. Behind blacked-out windows, the eccentric industrialist and former moviemaker descended into a private hell, battling desegregation, the Atomic Energy Commission and germs with equal fanatical fervor. He also created a gambling empire.

In Las Vegas in the 1940s, Hughes cut a dashing figure as a daredevil airman sporting a snap-brim Stetson. When he returned to stay in 1966, Hughes had over a half-billion dollars in cash from the sale of TransWorld Airlines. His first acquisition was the Desert Inn itself early in 1967.

Now safe from eviction, Hughes went on to purchase six other Nevada hotel-casinos. In Las Vegas, those purchases included the Sands, Castaways, Silver Slipper and Landmark, all now vanished or closed. Easily the largest gaming operator in Las Vegas, he sought also to acquire the Stardust but was thwarted by the Justice Department's Antitrust Division.

These investments cost him dearly as most of them lost extravagant sums of money. Traffickers in worthless mining claims bilked him of an additional twenty million dollars.

Publicly, the Hughes presence in Nevada was a triumph for the state's image, recently tarnished by revelations of organized crime involvement in gaming. Then-Governor Paul Laxalt was quoted to the effect that Hughes "added a degree of credibility to the state that it might have taken years of advertising to secure." Privately, only a handful of aides saw the madness at the center of the Hughes empire. Almost four years to the day after his arrival in Las Vegas, the aides carried Hughes' drug-wasted 115-pound frame down a fire escape and spirited him out of town. On his head perched a rakish new snap-brim Stetson.

Howard Hughes poses under one of his aircraft in the late 1950s.

ABOUT THE AUTHOR

Frank Wright 1938-2003

Frank Wright spent only about half his life in Las Vegas, but Las Vegas became his whole life. Originally a political scientist, he became the keeper of Las Vegas history, passionate in uncovering the truth; diplomatic yet firm in deflating the myth.

Born in Salt Lake City on June 15, 1938, he was educated at the University of Utah, and taught political science at the University of Montana before assuming a similar job at Nevada Southern University (now the University of Nevada, Las Vegas) in 1968.

He left the job in 1973 to pursue a doctorate degree, returned to Las Vegas and worked two years as hotel night manager at the famed Binion's Horseshoe Casino on Fremont Street, and was hired as curator of education at the Nevada Historical Society. He would work as a historian the rest of his days.

His duties included developing historical studies materials for school children. Once-legendary figures like trappers Joe Meek and Jim Beckworth had faded from the state's popular culture by 1983, when his booklet, *The Mountain Man — Early Explorers of Nevada* brought them back to life in a compact, yet realistic version, which children could appreciate. It was one of at least nine monographs Wright would publish to shake the dust off a colorful past.

Dorothy Ritenour, then employed by the Nevada Humanities Committee, approached Wright for help in developing a traveling program to enliven history studies throughout Southern Nevada. He served four years as a speaker for Humanities on the Road, where his storytelling ability, his bushy moustaches and weathered face, left a long-lasting impression on his listeners.

Wright and Ritenour became allies in efforts to preserve the vanishing historical buildings and sites of Las Vegas, a contribution recognized posthumously in 2004, when the city of Las Vegas gave his name to a pavilion in a downtown mini-park near a historic post office building.

The allies also became friends and, in February 1984, husband and wife. Dorothy Wright is now employed by Clark County Parks and Community Services.

Frank's projects sometimes touched the uncomfortable parts of Las Vegas history, as in 1994, when he curated an exhibit called "Eastside — Westside: Overcoming a Segregated Environment, 1940-1960." But they also celebrated some of Las Vegas' moments of self-sacrifice, as in the museum's permanent exhibit, "Las Vegas: The War Years."

Besides scripts for the *Nevada Yesterdays* pieces collected in this book, he wrote and narrated the TV/video series *Looking Back At Nevada* with the Cultural Division of Clark County Parks and Recreation. In recent years he served on the boards of the Las Vegas Springs Preserve, the Neon Museum and the city of Las Vegas Historic Preservation Commission; in earlier years he had helped guide such organizations as the Preservation Association of Clark County, the Southern Nevada Historical Society, and Allied Arts Council.

The *Las Vegas Review-Journal*'s staff in 2002 named him "Most Popular Male Las Vegan" in its annual "Best of Las Vegas" awards.

Wright retired February 2, 2002, and began work on this volume. He had been diagnosed with cancer in 2001, and not long after his retirement, there was a recurrence. Wright made a last-ditch effort to expedite his project, editing and polishing a number of the vignettes before the advancing illness forced him to hand off the final tasks to his wife. Wright died April 25, 2003, survived by Dorothy; a stepson, Christopher Ritenour; a brother, Robert Wright; four grandchildren; and a large body of carefully researched historical lore, much of which, without him, would have vanished forever.

ACKNOWLEDGMENTS

The family of Frank Wright and Stephens Press extend their thanks to the following people, who stand out among many who helped make this book possible.

Dr. Ed Baker of Seattle, who read the manuscript and encouraged its publication.

Ginger Bruner, of KNPR, who produced *Nevada Yesterdays.*

Michael Green, of the history department at the Community College of Southern Nevada, for continuing Frank's work writing *Nevada Yesterdays* scripts.

A. D. Hopkins, for his able editing and unwavering championship of *Nevada Yesterdays.*

David Millman, of the Nevada State Museum and Historical Society, for fact checking, photo selection, and general assistance.

Joe Thomson, for his able research of photos appropriate for this book.

Sue Campbell for the book design and production.

And, Tasha Cortez for timelines research.